Sew a Beautiful Window

SALLY COWAN

Published by

Krause Publications

700 E. State St.
Iola, WI 54990-0001
Telephone 715-445-2214
www.krause.com

Please call or write for our free catalog of publications. Our toll-free number to place an order or obtain a free catalog is 800-258-0929 or please use our regular business telephone, 715-445-2214.

Library of Congress Catalog Number: 2001090489

ISBN: 0-87349-255-2

Illustrations by Kurt Loftis, Kurtis Creative, Inc.
Photos by George McHendry, Photo-Graphics by McHendry, unless otherwise indicated.

Printed in the United States of America

It has often been said that the
"eyes are the window to the soul."
Perhaps our windows reflect a look
into our hearts.

Sally Cowan

Dedication

This book is dedicated to my brother, George McHendry, who did the photography for this and my first book, *Sew a Beautiful Home*. Working together as professionals made us realize that our love overrides any differences we might have had as young children. We discovered that family comes first. Also to my husband, Cary, who keeps me focused and, best of all, very spoiled.

A family portrait. Left to right: Sally, Mother, Daddy, and brother George McHendry.

Acknowledgments

The author, photographer, window treatment consultant, and illustrator make up a team of four. This book would not have been possible without each one being willing to be a team player.

Special thanks to Robin McCallister, George McHendry and Kurt Loftis.

Another member of the team is a very special person who has guided me through the process of writing two books. Without my editor from Krause Publications, Barbara Case, none of this would have been possible. She acts as a guiding light and I can't thank her enough for holding my feet to the fire when I needed it most.

There were many people who were willing to give us access to their "view from the inside." Thanks to the following people for sharing their creative window treatments, their expertise, and the warmth and love within their homes. And yes, their darling children and pets.

Renee Scott
Potter's House Christian
   Fellowship
Hosanna House
Rackley Rods
Debbie Shagnea
Erin Alderman, Alderman
   Interior Design
Jennifer Eccleston
Taylor Woodrow
   Communities Design
   Center

Marlene Frazier
Barbara K. Hoover Interiors
Donna Kauffman, Donna
   Kauffman Interiors
Chris and Kathe Swindel
Church of the Good
   Shepherd
Suzanne Suttles, Allied
   Member ASID
Robin St. Denis
Susan Weeks
Lisa Hardison, Designer's
   Workshop
Lamp Post Antiques
Ginger Wallace
FCCJ Window Treatment
   Design and Home
   Accessories classes
Karen Meyer
John and Paula Usry
Dal Shirah, installer along
   with Dave Polscer
Missy Chapman
David and Pam Blumberg
Pam Edmiston
Lillian Ward

I am also thankful to the companies that provided products and equipment:
Superior Threads
Sulky of America
Robinson-Anton
Babylock U.S.A.
Pfaff
Husqvarna Viking

You learn very quickly when writing a book that "no man (or in this case, no woman) is an island." It takes a whole team.

Robin McCallister, consultant.

Photo by Helene McHendry.

George McHendry, the photographer. But not just any photographer – my brother.

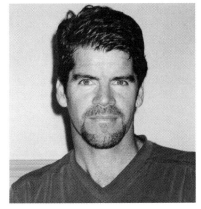

Kurt Loftis, an award-winning illustrator who has worked with me for many years on various projects and is someone I have always been able to count on.

Table of Contents

"View" 4

"View" 5

"View" 6

"View" 8

"View" 9

"View" 10

"View" 11

"View" 12

Introduction

While writing my first book, *Sew a Beautiful Home*, I became a true advocate of home decorating. I had never been far from home decorating projects in my personal life, but garment sewing had always been my first love. Well, that has changed. After sewing for people for 30 years, I have found sewing for a window or a bed is so much easier. Windows and beds don't change size (unless you buy a new one), and they don't complain. The satisfaction of decorating an area in a home that will be shared by many is a wonderful privilege.

As your family sits around the kitchen table, you can't help but notice the window treatments that add warmth and atmosphere to that area. The definition of a window is "an opening in a building for admitting light and air, usually having a pane of glass." Notice the definition says nothing about a curtain. We add curtains to give us privacy from those looking in, yet we want curtains that will allow us to look out and see the world. The curtains are visible from the outside and they should reflect the love and warmth shared on the inside.

The subtitle for *Sew a Beautiful Window* could very easily be "Instruction and Inspiration." After you read the instructions, I hope you will be inspired to go a step further and create the window treatment that fits your family and your lifestyle.

This book will help you plan your window style, suggest various pleats and headings, discuss the importance of color, fabrics, and so much more. After you understand the type of window you want to treat, you will find solutions to many challenging windows. To make your decisions a little easier, you'll find many examples of valances, swags, jabots, and the potpourri of window treatments that go the extra mile. Naturally I didn't leave out the essential details such as window hardware, equipment, cutting, matching, measuring, lining, and hemming.

The featured window treatments include step-by-step instructions and most are followed by inspirational variations based on that particular window treatment. This gives you the option to personalize each window treatment in your home. The sky's the limit.

The first step – getting started – is always the hardest. Together we will walk through each "pane"-less step so that the dream of decorating your own windows can be realized.

As in everything I do, I incorporate some humor and add a bit of history. I think we take things far too seriously. When it comes to window treatments, the best treatment we can give ourselves is to "lighten up." In other words, let your light shine through.

Your eyes are the windows of your soul. Your homes are the windows of your life.

Sally Cowan

P.S. Because windows come in all sizes, it would be impossible to give exact measurements and fabric amounts for each and every window treatment. Keep in mind, there are many commercial patterns to help you figure out how much fabric is necessary for a particular window. The patterns also list the notions needed. I use sample measurements for illustrative purposes, but your measurements will, of course, be different to fit your window.

View 1

Windows With Perspective

Windows originally were just glass and a wooden frame. A window was considered a necessary opening that let fresh air in and fireplace smoke out. It has become much more than that in the 21st century. Let's take a minute and give some thought to the historical background of window treatments.

Historically, windows spoke for themselves. A window was part of the architectural design and didn't need much help – it was simply a window. But that has changed. As far back as medieval Europe, windows were covered with a wooden shutter to provide protection from the outside world. Very few people had the means to add window dressings to their homes. In reality, only the nobility were able to afford them.

During the Middle Ages, designs became richer and bolder. It wasn't uncommon to see beautiful rich embroidery in homes of the day. Curtains became a common addition to the home in the 16th century in England, when windows were covered with one large piece of fabric rather than two pieces as is common today. The Italians and French led the way in terms of curtains that hung in pairs, well short of the floor.

The 17th century was a turning point in home decorating, which started to include curtains, wall hangings, and even the furnishings. But curtains were still not seen everywhere until the 18th century. So what happened in the 18th century? The answer is simple: Fabric became much more accessible. There was an abundance of printed cotton chintzes, silks, velvets, brocades, and mixed fabrics such as silk/linen blends. By the 19th century both curtains and draperies played a major role in interior home decorating. Words we are familiar with today were just starting to be used: swag, cornice, fringe, tassel, pole, finial, bracket, and molding.

At the beginning of the 20th century the window styles were simpler. Heavy, ornate fabrics took a back seat. There was another major change during this time – manufacturers made it possible to *buy* curtains rather than make them. Not only that, but they were washable.

What a fabulous concept! Also at this time, there was an abundance of fabric patterns and colors available to choose from. For a time after World War II, home decorating hit an all-time low, but that was understandable – food was more important.

So here we are, in the 21st century when fabrics, information, styles, patterns, and hardware are found in hundreds of stores. We are free to personalize our windows any way we want. That's what I call freedom.

My Point of View

The best result is when the room doesn't look decorated.

View 2

Glossary

*L*ike any foreign language, when you understand the words, you understand the process. With some of these terms under your belt, you will be able to converse much more easily with your fabric store or decorator. Besides, it makes you look very smart!

Apron: A decorative molding under the windowsill.

Architrave: The wooden molding around a door or window.

Banner valance: A series of fabric triangles attached to a mounting board or threaded on a rod. Also called a handkerchief valance.

Balloon shade: A window treatment of shirred or gathered fabric drawn up into billowy folds. Can also be called a balloon valance.

Baseboard: A narrow border that runs along the base of a wall where it meets the floor. Often made from wood. Also called skirting board.

Bay window: A three-sided (or more) window that protrudes from the exterior wall of a house.

Bias: 45° diagonal to the direction of the weave in fabric.

Blackout lining: A three-layer fabric consisting of two layers of cotton and one layer of opaque material. This lining helps completely block out the light.

Bow window: Bay windows that are semicircular.

Box pleats: Pleats formed by folding the fabric to the backside of the pleat in a "box" shape.

Braid: A flat decorative trim that can be used to embellish window treatments. Gimps and woven ribbons can fall in this category.

Brocade: A rich fabric with an embossed design, usually gold or silver.

Buckram: A coarse cotton, hemp, or linen cloth stiffened with glue or a glue-like substance used in the header of pleated draperies. Buckram can give lasting shape to a valance. Also called crinoline.

Bump: Cotton lining added to curtain panels to add body to a curtain.

Café curtain: A short curtain hung on a rod.

Café rod: A slim curtain rod.

Calico: A plain-weave fabric made from raw unbleached cotton.

Cartridge pleats: Cylindrical pleats that are a great alternative for pleated valances and long curtains.

Cascade: A rippling or showering fall of fabric seen in draperies. Also called a jabot.

Cased heading: A simple pocket created as a heading into which the curtain rod is inserted.

Casement window: A hinged window operated by a crank mechanism that can open in or out.

Casing: A fabric pocket to encase a curtain rod or elastic for gathering. Usually made by folding fabric over twice and stitching. Basically, a hem with open ends.

Chenille: Very soft fabric made with fluffy cotton yarns.

Chintz: A floral printed cotton fabric.

Cleat: A metal or plastic hook placed at the side of the window to hold the cords of a shade or drape.

Continental rod: Flat curtain rods that protrude from the wall to add depth and interest to rod pocket treatments. The most common widths are 2-1/2" and 4-1/2".

Cornice: An ornamental band for covering a curtain rod. It is made of a rigid panel covered with fabric.

Cornice board: A horizontal board used to support the cornice.

Cornice pole: A pole with rings. Often used for heavy curtains.

Cotton: A natural fiber fabric made from fibers in the boll of the cotton plant.

Curtain: A window covering, usually unlined and made from lightweight fabric.

Curtain drop: The length of a curtain from the hanging system to the bottom edge.

Cut drop: The finished bottom of a curtain, plus allowances for hems or headings.

Cut length: The length plus allowances for hems and seams or headers.

Cut width: The width plus allowances for side hems.

Damask: A woven fabric made from wool, silk, or cotton. The special weave gives the fabric a raised appearance.

Double hem: A hem where the fabric is turned

over twice, usually by the same amount, so the raw edge is completely encased.

Double-hung window: The most common type of window, consisting of an upper and lower sash. Both sashes move up and down.

Dowel rod: A slender rod placed inside the fabric pocket to raise or lower the shade. It creates neat and tidy folds. Used for Roman shades.

Drapery: A window covering, usually lined, made of mid- to heavyweight fabrics, and extending to the floor. A cloth, fabric, and textile. Hangings arranged in loose folds.

Drapery return: *see Return.*

Drop length: The distance from the top of the object to where you want the fabric to end.

Fabric panel: The result of all fabric widths sewn together.

Facing: A piece of fabric that strengthens the main piece of fabric.

Fascia: A vertical board that covers the curtain heading.

Festoon: A fabric treatment that is fixed at the top of the window.

Finial: An ornamental projection on the end of a curtain rod or pole.

Finished length: The length of the curtain after all the hems and headers are sewn.

Finished drop line: The place where the curtain stops.

Finished width: The width of the fabric after all seams and side hems are sewn.

Flat fell seam: A seam that gives extra strength to a seam.

French door: Doors with multiple windowpanes.

French pleats: *see Pencil pleats.*

French seam: A way of stitching fabric together with the seam hidden from view. Used on sheer fabrics.

Gather: Bringing fabric into a tighter position to add fullness.

Gathering tape: A heading tape that creates a ruffled effect.

Gingham: Plain-weave cotton cloth with a checked pattern.

Goblet pleats: A pleat that is pushed out and filled with curtain lining instead of folded inward. So named because the pleat resembles a goblet.

Grain: The direction of the threads in fabric. Can be crosswise or lengthwise.

Grommet: Brass or chrome hole reinforcements at the top of a curtain. Available at most hardware stores. A grommet tool is needed to insert these holes.

Header: The extra fabric above the curtain rod pocket. Usually for decorative purposes.

Heading: The very top of the curtain. The heading can include ties, rings, tape, and other treatments.

Heading tape: *see Pleater tape.*

Hem: Turning under and stitching a raw edge.

Holdback: An ornament used to hold the curtain off the window when open. Can be wood, glass, porcelain, or metal.

Interlining: A soft fabric placed between the fabric and the lining that provides insulation.

Jabot: *see Cascade.*

Jamb: The molding around the window. The vertical molding is the side jamb, the horizontal is the head jamb.

Lath: The top of a shade is fitted to this piece of wood, which is usually 2" x 1". The lath can be attached to the wall, ceiling, or window frame.

Leading edge: Where the drapery panels overlap in the center of a two-way traverse rod. The overlap that occurs when the drapes are pulled in a closed position. Also called overlap edge.

Lining: Fabric layer (usually made from cotton sateen) placed on the back of curtains to protect them from light and dust.

Mitering: A diagonal seam that joins two pieces of fabric at a corner.

Mullion: The vertical strip of wood that separates the panes of glass in a window.

Overlap: *see Leading edge.*

Palladian window: A series of windows with an arch on top. Also called arched windows.

Pattern repeat: The distance between identical motifs in a pattern. The total measurement of one complete design. Knowing the distance between the pattern repeats on the fabric is vital in order to join patterned fabric and also is key in determining how much extra fabric to buy.

Pelmet: A panel that covers the top of a curtain. Can be made of wood or covered with fabric. Also called a cornice.

Pencil pleats: Pleats created using a special tape sewn to the heading of a valance or drapery. When the tape is drawn up, it creates a narrow row of folds resembling a row of pencils laid side by side.

Picture window: A large window with fixed panes.

Pinch pleats: A style of pleat, usually triple folded, used at the header of a curtain or valance.

Piping: A decorative edge made from bias-cut fabric strips that cover a cord.

Pleat: A crease or fold.

Pleater tape: A ready-made strip sewn to the top of a curtain and attached to the hanging system. Pleater tape is available in various styles. Also called heading tape.

Poplin: Cotton fabric with a corded surface.

Railroading: Turning fabric on its side so the width becomes the length. Used to eliminate seams for sewing valances, cornices, or ruffles.

Recess window: A window set back into a wall. The curtain is often hung inside the recess.

Repeat: *see Pattern repeat.*

Return: The measurement from the front of the rod to the wall. Also called a drapery return.

Rod: A metal fixture that holds the curtain instead of a pole. Rods may have cords and overlap arms.

Rod pocket: The flat casing that runs the width of the panel. The curtain rod is inserted in the rod pocket.

Roman shade: A window shade made from fabric that hangs flat when down but folds like an accordion when raised. Can also be mock.

Rosette: Decorative trim shaped like a rose. Often used with swags in window treatments.

Scallops: Deep round curves. Often seen at the bottom edge of café curtains.

Sconce: A wall-mounted fixture that is great for draping fabric through.

Seam: The join where two pieces of fabrics are sewn together

Seam allowance: An extra amount of fabric used when joining fabric.

Self-pelmet: A piece of fabric stitched to the top of a curtain to make it appear to be separate.

Selvage: A finished edge that runs the length of the fabric piece.

Sheers: A window treatment made with sheer fabric that allows daylight in while providing limited privacy.

Silk: A very strong, yet soft fabric made from threads produced by silkworms.

Slot heading: *see Rod pocket.*

Smocked pleats: A heading that resembles a hand-worked smocked pattern.

Spring-tension rod: An adjustable rod that fits inside the window frame. The internal spring makes it possible to adjust this rod. Often used for café curtains and sheer treatments.

Support: A pole or track that holds a curtain or shade.

Swag: A window treatment that can be hung on a rod or attached to a mounting board. Swags can be formally pleated or casually gathered. A length of fabric loosely draped over a rod can be dressed to form a casual style swag treatment. It takes a little tweaking but can be made with little or no sewing.

Tail: The fabric that hangs from the end of a swag. Can be shaped or free falling.

Tapestry: Machine-woven fabric that looks hand-woven.

Thermal lining: Fabric that is layered with aluminum on one side for the purpose of insulation.

Tieback: Fabric, rope, ribbon, trim, or other materials used to hold the curtain back.

Undercurtain: *see Lining.*

Valance: A top treatment that can stand alone or be mounted over draperies.

Voile: Light plain-weave cotton fabric often used for sheer curtains.

Weights: Small metal discs placed in the hem of a curtain to make it hang better.

Width: The distance between the selvages of all fabrics.

View 3

Windows of
Opportunity

Planning Your Style:
A "Pane"-less Thought Process

With all things, the first step is the hardest. By using a step-by-step approach, you will be able to make it over the first hurdle. Perhaps at this point it would be even better to take baby steps. Let me help you get out of the starting gate without tripping or, even worse, hitting the gate.

Take a few minutes to sit down and decide which of these issues are important to you. Some are phrased as a question and some are statements to make you think.

If your pet likes to sit in the window, be sure to select a window treatment that's easily washable.

Consider:
* Your budget. How much do you want to spend?
* What style do you hope to achieve?
* What style furnishings are in the room?
* What colors do you favor?
* The size of the window.
* Fabric textures. Visit a fabric store to get an idea of the variety of textures available.
* How will the window treatment look from the outside?
* How much light do you want to come through the window?
* How important is the view from the window?
* Do you need the window treatment to mask a problem window?
* Is privacy an issue?
* Do you open and close the window?
* If the window is in a child's room, child safety is an important factor.
* Do you want a formal or informal look?
* Will the window coverings be lined or unlined?
* Do you have a dog or cat that likes to sit in the window?
* What kind of heading do you want?

Children's rooms are fun to decorate, but remember to consider safety when making decorating decisions.

* Do you have a view you love to look at on a daily basis?
* Do you want natural light to shine in your home office area?

Is natural light an option, or will you depend on artificial light?

* What kind of drapery hardware will work best?
* To tieback or not to tieback, that is the question.
* Consider using blinds or shades.
* Give yourself a deadline.
* Give yourself a deadline
* Give yourself a deadline. (I think you get the point.)
* Most of all, have fun.

As you start thinking about your window treatment style, keep in mind that good design and understated elegance never go out of style.

The finished product should be a room that doesn't look overly decorated. You want the room to reflect you and your family, not look like a museum showroom. If you give some thought to the points listed above and plan well, you can't help but have a successful outcome with your window treatments.

It would be a shame to hide this pleasant view with the wrong window treatment.

There are many similarities in how you dress yourself and how you dress your windows. Look through your closet and note what color is most prominent. Obviously, that is a color you like.

Before you start on any decorating project, decisions have to be made. Do you want a country look? A look of luxury? Windows that make a bold statement? A classic look or windows that are light and airy? Here are some questions to ask yourself to help you decide what style would work best for you.

* Do you like dark wood, needlepoint, velvets, and stained glass windows? Do you like patterned rugs and basically feel that "more is better?" If so, choose **Victorian**.
* Do you like fine wood, muted shades, high chests, and drop-leaf tables? Is "simple" your middle name? Choose **Colonial**.
* Do you like Art Deco, leather chairs, chrome, glass, and exotic colors? Choose **Modern**.
* Do you like lace curtains, informality, pine floors, and exposed beams? Have you always dreamed of a rustic, simple, charming place? Choose **Country**.
* Do you like quilts, hooked rugs, crocks, and bright colors? Choose **American Country**.
* Do you like clutter to surround you? Pine furniture, throw blankets, and country pictures? Choose **English Country**.
* Do you like tile floors, provincial prints, and walnut furniture? Choose **French Country**.
* Do you like a little of all of the above? Choose **Eclectic**.

Types of Headings

The type of heading you choose will help determine your style.

Pinch pleats are also called triple pleats or French pleats. This type of heading will give you a very traditional style. The pinch pleat is actually three small pleats grouped together at regular intervals. To achieve the proper fullness, allow 2-1/2 to 3 times the width for fullness. Pinch pleats work well when the curtains are interlined.

Pencil pleats are a narrow row of folds resembling a row of pencils laid side by side. The easiest way to make pencil pleats is with pleater tape. This tape comes in a variety of lengths and the most common widths are 2" and 4". Allow 2-1/2 to 3 times the track length for fullness. The heading is created by sewing the tape to the heading of a valance or drapery.

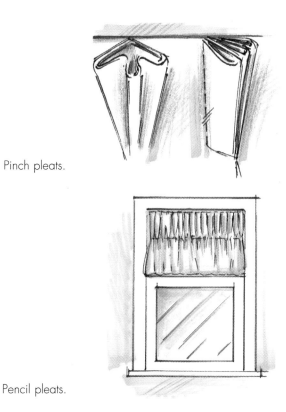

Pinch pleats.

Pencil pleats.

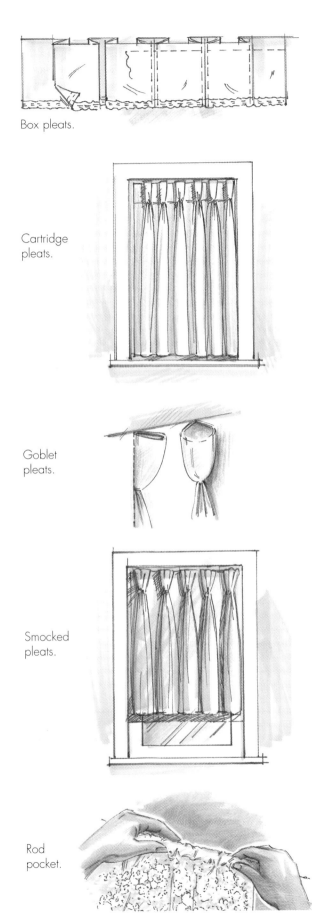

Box pleats.

Cartridge pleats.

Goblet pleats.

Smocked pleats.

Rod pocket.

Box pleats are often used when the curtain stays in a fixed position. This type of pleat is made by folding the fabric to the backside of the pleat. By adding a valance, you will accomplish a neat and tidy look. A fabric that creases well, such as a linen weave or cotton, will help maintain the shape of the box pleat. Allow 3 times the track length for fullness.

Cartridge pleats are cylindrical shaped pleats. This style pleat is an alternative to pinch pleats. Allow 2-1/2 to 3 times the track length for fullness.

Goblet pleats are similar to pinch pleats but the top of the pleat is not brought together as a triple fold. The top of a goblet pleat is stuffed with an interlining so the top will stay full. A border across the top of the fabric gives this heading a beautiful finish. Allow 3 times the track length for fullness.

Smocked pleats create a smocked look that's great for valances and curtains. You can use standard hooks placed in one or two rows of the hook pockets. Allow 2-1/2 times the track length for fullness. Using pleater tapes makes smocked pleats a breeze (see page 112).

A **rod pocket heading** is just that. The fabric is folded down at the top to create a pocket the rod can travel through. Lightweight to medium weight fabrics are your best choice.

Tabbed headings can be made with eyelets, ropes, ties, tabs, buttons, rings, or any other shape you fancy.

Tabbed heading.

Window Shapes

Without walking around the house and looking, can you describe each window in each of your rooms? Probably not, but before you decide how to "treat" your windows, I suggest you pull up a chair and look at the window or windows you are about to dress. Think about:

* the shape,
* the proportions,
* the amount of light that comes in the window,
* the view, or lack of view.

Windows fall into three basic categories: square, landscape (wider than tall), and portrait (taller than wide).

Obviously there can be many combinations of these three shapes. While you are looking at your window, consider whether you will make a pair of curtains, a single curtain, use a tieback (because you love the view), or use blinds and curtains together.

Landscape windows are usually covered with curtains that separate in the middle. If you decide to also use a heading, be sure to keep it simple. You want to avoid making the window look top heavy. The old rule "keep it simple" is still the best advice.

Portrait-shaped windows.

This antique store window is a perfect example of a square-shaped window.

Four portrait–shaped windows create a landscape-shaped effect.

Bay windows.

Double-hung windows.

Double-hung windows with drapes and a valance.

Awning/Sash Crank Windows – Windows that crank to the outside and open from the bottom.

Bay Windows – A grouping of windows that protrude to the outside. They often have a built-in seat that gives you a fabulous place to read a book or enjoy what lies outside your window. Bay windows usually consist of a group of three or more windows set at an angle to each other in a recessed area.

Bow Windows – Unlike bay windows that are set at an angle, bow windows are on a curve. They also project to the outside and often have a window seat built in. Bow windows are also called a circular bay.

Casement Windows – Casement windows open by a crank mechanism. Because they can open in or out, they are set on a hinge. Casement windows call for a window treatment that completely clears the window. Because these windows can be cranked outward, your best treatment choices are draperies or curtains on rings. By adding a cornice or valance you can soften the look.

Double-Hung Windows – Double-hung windows consist of an upper and lower sash. It would be a rare house that didn't have this type of window. The sashes slide up and down. Window treatment choices are endless for double-hung windows. Traditional swags and cascades are a classic favorite. If you are more adventuresome, consider Roman shades or more casual options such as pleated panels, panels on rings, or rod-pocket curtains. If you want to dress this up slightly, add a valance or cornice as shown in the illustration.

French Doors – Doors with multiple windowpanes. The doors often open onto a porch. French doors add a touch of elegance. Sheers are often used as a standard treatment but also consider a banner valance as shown in the photo.

Palladian Window (also called arched) – Windows with an arch shape on top. The arched window became popular in the 1700s. This particular window has always evoked a feeling of grandeur. The arched top can be left untreated, or you can choose to treat all or part of the window because of privacy or light exposure issues.

French doors.

Palladian windows.

A banner valance on a French door.

A square window treatment on a Palladian window. Because the fabric is sheer, the arch shape is still visible.

A picture window.

Sliding glass doors.

Picture Window – A large window with fixed panes.

Sliding Glass Doors – Doors that form a wall of glass. Because they are opened and closed often, it takes a little more planning when choosing the window treatment for sliding glass doors. You want something that is easy to operate. Vertical blinds are certainly a good option but you are not limited to them. Draperies on a one-way traverse rod allow you to open the drapes quickly and have them stack back, out of your way.

No matter what kind of windows you have, they can add immeasurable beauty to any room. With that said, windows can also stump many well-meaning home decorators. If you love the view and aren't concerned about privacy, consider not adding any treatment. However, if you're like most of us and would rather the world not see every move you make, add window treatments that enhance the window and the room.

Palladian windows add grandeur to the ballroom.

My Point of View

Can you imagine life without windows? If you want to reduce your stress level, find more time to sit at a window and peer out at the world and all its beauty. No time, you say? Make time.

View 4
Solutions for Challenging Windows

While writing this book, I was tempted to ignore those difficult windows (sometimes called window-pains), but knew that wouldn't be fair to readers. Therefore, various challenging windows are addressed in this chapter, along with solutions.

In every home, there's probably at least one window that just doesn't look right or that you don't particularly like. If you have a window like this, try one of the following methods to camouflage it.

Bring curtains together at the top and add tiebacks to make the window look narrower.

Extend the rod well beyond the sides of the window to make the window look wider.

To make a wide window look narrower, bring the top of the curtains together (or almost together) and add tiebacks.

To make a narrow window look wider or to maximize the amount of light coming in, position the curtain rod beyond the sides of the window. When open, the draperies will stack back off the window, allowing the maximum amount of light to come in.

To make a window look taller, install the hardware higher than normal above the window. This creates the illusion of height in the room and is especially helpful in a small or low-ceilinged room.

To make a window look shorter, use a long swag or valance. It is rare that you would want to do this because a window looks best when it appears higher.

Mount the rod considerably above the window to make the window look taller.

A long swag or valance can make a window look shorter.

Although Palladian (arched) windows are lovely and add luxury to any room, they present a challenge when adding window treatments. These tall windows with an arch on top can be wide or narrow. If you aren't concerned about privacy, I suggest leaving the window bare. But if privacy is an issue, here are some suggestions:

* Below the top arch, hang a Roman shade or a valance.
* Place wood blinds on the lower portion of the window.
* Buy or have custom made, blinds that fit the arched area.

Wood blinds on the lower part of a Palladian window.

* Below the top arch, hang swags using decorative finials.
* Install a very sheer window treatment over the entire window, still revealing the shape of the arch.
* Or you can decorate the arch itself.

Accent the arch by decorating it.

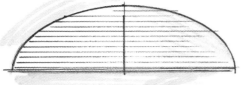

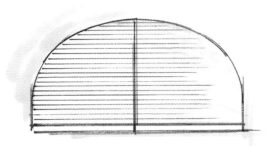

Blinds that fit the shape of the window.

A swag hung below the arch reveals the lovely arch shape.

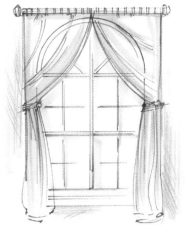

Using sheer fabric allows the arch shape to show.

Picture windows can be softened by using simple blinds and a fringed valance.

Angle windows with stagecoach valances.

The valance and drapes add a touch of elegance to this door.

Picture Windows

Picture windows create a feeling of vastness and provide a wonderful view, but their size can present a decorating challenge.

Consider using sheers across a picture window with a tailored valance, or vertical blinds with a valance. A sweeping swag with jabots can be very effective, as can a cornice board with stationary panels.

Angle Windows

Angle windows are two identical windows positioned on each side of a corner.

For windows like these, I recommend using a simple treatment such as a stagecoach valance at the top and leaving the bottom open (or use mini-blinds for privacy).

These windows could also be treated as a bay window (see page 22).

Sliding Glass Doors

Sliding glass doors can be perplexing because you want them to be accessible.

Vertical blinds have been a simple solution for years. When closed, the blinds conceal the doors, yet are easy to open when the door is in use. To soften the look, consider a valance over the doors.

Also consider using a decorative pole, making curtains with ring tops, pulling the curtains open during the day with tiebacks, or using swags and jabots.

Vertical blinds on sliding glass doors.

Bay Windows

What should you do with that lovely bay window? You know, the window that convinced you to buy the house. Bay windows need to be incorporated into the overall scheme of things.

Options for bay windows include multiple throw swags and/or decorative hardware, balloon valances, a continuous box-pleated valance, or swags that combine various fabric prints.

Swags.

Balloon valances on bay windows.

A continuous box-pleated valance.

French Doors

French doors can consist of one, two, four doors, or more. Perhaps you have stayed in a quaint hotel in France and loved the French doors that led out to the porch or garden. Every time you see French doors, you think about that romantic once-in-a-lifetime trip. If you are fortunate to have these doors in your home, there are many ways to create a feeling of privacy without blocking out the light.

Open these full drapes during the day and close them at night.

Mini blinds work well on any door with glass.

Try balloon shades mounted on the door, or mount mini-blinds to cover the glass section of the door.

Traditional drapes mounted on a conventional or decorative rod can be pulled open during the day and closed at night.

Make a curtain with a rod pocket that can be gathered on a simple rod. Using sheer fabrics creates a "Paris" illusion.

Swags draped above the doors can be just the right finishing touch.

A gathered valance above the doors adds a decorative touch without overwhelming the effect of the doors.

Sheers create a luminous effect.

These swags are draped above the doors at the lovely Hosanna House.

A gathered valance adds a subtle touch of decorating.

These elegant drapes enhance the look of the French doors.

Sidelights

These long windows are usually next to a door. Here are two examples of how to handle these windows, but feel free to let your imagination run wild.

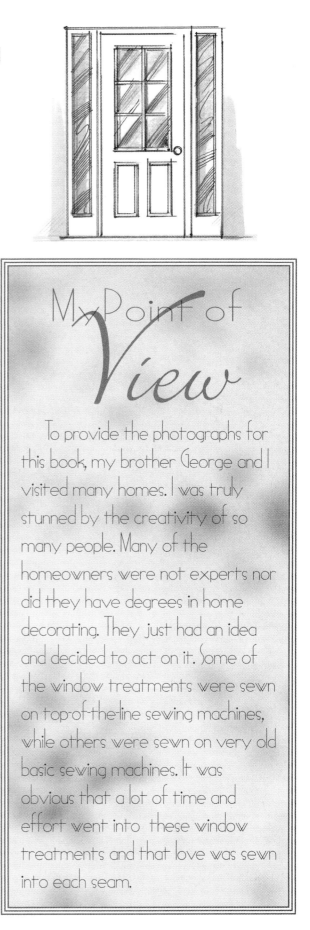

Here, a straight panel with an attached valance and tasseled trim covers the sidelight.

Sidelights can be covered with a narrow set of blinds.

My Point of View

To provide the photographs for this book, my brother George and I visited many homes. I was truly stunned by the creativity of so many people. Many of the homeowners were not experts nor did they have degrees in home decorating. They just had an idea and decided to act on it. Some of the window treatments were sewn on top-of-the-line sewing machines, while others were sewn on very old basic sewing machines. It was obvious that a lot of time and effort went into these window treatments and that love was sewn into each seam.

View 5

Choosing the
Right Fabric

Fabric, fabric, and more fabric. Fabrics do make a difference. Before walking into a fabric store and becoming overwhelmed, look through magazines and get an idea of the type of fabrics you prefer. Consider the texture, the color tones, geometric patterns, and fabric content.

There are many home decorating books that suggest do's and don'ts for fabric selection but I don't think there are any rules when it comes to choosing the fabric. If the fabric produces the look you want, then use it. After all, home decorating is about fabric – the feel, weight, and overall impression it has on your psyche. Creating your own window treatment gives you the opportunity to stitch in your personality and the love you have for your home. The fabric you choose will indeed make an ordinary window extraordinary.

Points to Consider When Selecting Fabric

* Most fabrics for home decorating are 54" wide.
* Most decorator fabrics are on a cardboard roll. Unroll a couple yards before purchasing the fabric.
* Bring colors from the room with you, such as a pillow or paint color. Stand back and look at the fabric.
* Over buy rather than under buy the fabric. Fabric from a different bolt can have color differences.
* Check for flaws as the fabric is being measured to be cut.

* Decorator fabrics have a high thread count so they hold up longer.
* It's not necessary to preshrink decorator fabric.
* Bring accurate measurements of the window with you.
* If allowed, carry the fabric outside and look at it in natural light.
* Don't buy a print that's too "busy."
* If stripes make you dizzy, avoid them.

Types of Fabric

Natural Fiber Fabrics

Cotton

The simple definition: An absorbent fiber made from the cotton plant. Cotton is the basis for many fiber combinations and is often referred to as the fiber of a thousand faces because it comes in an endless variety of colors and weights. Cotton blends well with many other fibers that make it desirable. It drapes well, has little elasticity, rarely shrinks, conducts heat well, does not sun rot, and accepts dyes.

Heavy cotton is very suitable for a variety of window treatments, including floor length drapes. Lighter, loosely woven cottons such as lace or muslin work well for drapes that allow the light to shine in.

Care tips: Wash or dry clean. Iron, using high temperatures.

Sewing tips: Select the sewing machine needle size according to the weight of the fabric. Loosen the tension on your machine when stitching. Check your sewing machine manual for the proper stitch length.

Linen

The simple definition: Fabric made from a flax plant. Linen can be of various weights. Linen dries quickly, resists moths, dyes well, doesn't stretch, and does not sun rot.

Linen works well for tailored window treatments because once the pleats are pressed, the creases hold tightly.

Care tips: Dry clean. Iron, using high temperatures.

Sewing tips: Use size 60/8 to 90/14 needles. Polyester thread is your best choice.

Silk

The simple definition: Fiber made by silkworms. Silk drapes well, resists wrinkling, has little static buildup, resists mildew, and does not sag. When silk is dyed, the colors are bold and bright. According to legend, a Chinese princess discovered silk accidentally. As she was sitting under a tree sipping tea, a cocoon dropped into her cup. The heat made it possible to unwind the fiber, which seemed to be continuous. By 2,600 B.C. silkworms were being raised and fed like kings and queens.

Because silk drapes so well, it works wonderfully for making casual swags. Silk needs to be lined to give it durability.

Care tips: Dry clean only. Iron, using medium temperatures.

Sewing tips: Use cotton or silk thread and fine pins. Baste with silk thread to avoid any imprints in the fabric.

Synthetic Fiber Fabrics

Damask

The simple definition: A reversible, flat fabric that is a combination of plain and satin weaves. Damask can be woven with silk, linen, cotton, rayon, or other fibers. Heavy damasks are often used when making formal draperies. Don't use damask to achieve a light, airy affect.

Care tips: Read the care label at the end of the fabric bolt. More than likely, dry cleaning would be your best choice.

Sewing tips: Use size 70/10 to 90/14 needles. Damask is best sewn with a polyester or cotton-wrapped polyester thread. Instead of tracing paper, use chalk or temporary marking pens.

Chintz

The simple definition: A tightly woven cotton fabric with a glazed finish. Chintz is primarily used for draperies, cushions, or slipcovers. Consider lining chintz to avoid sun damage. Chintz can be quilted, embossed, or smooth. Commonly called "polished cotton."

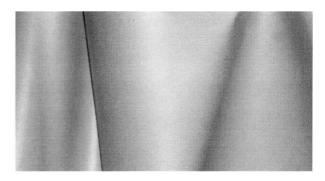

Chintz works well for cloud or balloon shades. Don't use this fabric for any window treatment that requires a lot of drape.

Care tips: Because of the glazed finish, I recommend dry cleaning this fabric. To find out if the finish is permanent, apply a drop of iodine to a small swatch. If it turns blue, it isn't; if it turns brown, it is.

Sewing tip: Use a sharp needle to penetrate the crisp surface.

Muslin

The simple definition: A soft woven cotton. Muslin can be bleached or unbleached, lightweight or heavyweight. It is inexpensive and can be used for simple draperies in a relaxed interior.

Care tips: Hand wash in cold water only, as muslin has a tendency to shrink. Be sure to wash before using.

Sewing tips: Use a rotary cutter for a clean cut. Use size 60/8 to 80/12 needles and cotton-wrapped polyester thread.

Polyester

The simple definition: A synthetic filament fiber made from petroleum by-products. Polyester has a tendency not to "breathe." The making process starts with hard polyester chips that are heated until they melt, then the liquid polyester is extruded through spinnerets, forming filaments.

Polyester resists wrinkling and moths. The ideal fabric is a combination of polyester and cotton blend. It works well for draperies when the fabric is crisp and can also be used to achieve gathers, soft folds, or ruffles.

Care tips: Wash or dry clean. Iron, using low temperatures.

Sewing tips: Use ballpoint needles and 100% polyester thread.

Voile

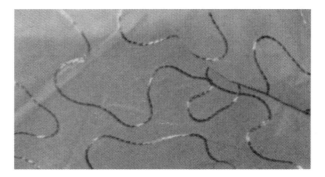

The simple definition: Fabric made from highly twisted natural and synthetic fibers, resulting in a fabric that is lightweight and crisp. Voile is often a cotton/polyester blend.

Voile can be used to make sheers that will help diffuse light and offer a little extra privacy. A self-lined voile will also make a beautiful swag and jabot treatment.

Care tips: Iron on a low setting. If washing, use a short wash cycle and wash in cold water.

Sewing tips: Use size 60/8 to 70/10 needles and extra-fine cotton-wrapped polyester thread. Because the fabric is delicate, use very fine pins to avoid pulling the fabric.

Taffeta

The simple definition: A tightly woven fabric with a crosswise rib that gives it a crisp appearance. It used to be very stiff but is now more pliable because it is combined with other fibers such as cotton, acetate, rayon, or polyester. Taffeta creases easily and can be tricky to use.

Taffeta used for draperies and valances, with beautiful trims and tassels, can create a great look in a formal room. Avoid using acetate taffetas near water, such as in a bathroom for a shower curtain or window valance.

Care tips: Press from the wrong side, using a press cloth and brown paper strips to avoid seam impressions on the outside. Water or steam can leave water marks that will not come out.

Sewing tips: Use size 60/8 to 80/12 needles and cotton-wrapped polyester thread. Use fine needles instead of pins.

Velvet

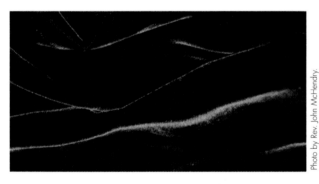

Photo by Rev. John McHendry.

The simple definition: A nap or pile fabric, with short pile on the front on a woven background. It is made mainly with silk or rayon pile and a cotton back. It can be all silk or woven of cotton, linen, rayon, and wool. In the past, velvet has been associated with more formal settings but can now be seen in a variety of applications such as curtains, bedding, and the like.

Care tips: Dry clean and steam, but never press. Brush away loose dirt with a vacuum.

Sewing tips: Use size 60/8 to 80/12 needles.

For silk velvets use mercerized cotton thread, otherwise use cotton-wrapped polyester thread. Mark with chalk or temporary marking pens.

Sheers

The simple definition: A lightweight, transparent fabric. This can include voile and lace. The fabric diffuses light and works great in conjunction with shades or blinds. There has always been the sense of privacy when using sheers.

Photo courtesy of Graber (Hand-Carved Wood Ware by Springs Window Fashions), Middleton, Wis.

Sheer fabric can be printed too.

Sheer fabrics have long been a part of French window treatments. No French country décor would be complete without a traditional swath of lace at the windows. Sheers can be formal, romantic, whimsical, and even tailored.

Care tips: Depending on the fiber content, sheer fabrics can usually be washed. Be sure to follow the manufacturer's instructions.

Sewing tips: Use size 60/8 to 70/10 needles and an extra-fine cotton-wrapped polyester thread. Don't mark with wax. Use French seams on the edges to enclose the seams.

Rayon

The simple definition: The oldest manmade fiber made from recycled cellulose. Rayon is a great fabric for draperies because of its drape-ability, softness, resistance to moths and static electricity, and economical price. But rayon has a tendency not to hold its shape, so is not suitable for pleated drapes. Because it drapes so well, it works well for simple valances or swags. In Britain, rayon is called viscose.

Care tips: Check the label on the bolt of cloth. Often you are instructed to wash before cutting. Use a mild detergent and hand wash in lukewarm water. Rinse thoroughly. Press on the wrong side, using a medium temperature.

Sewing tips: Use size 60/8 to 120/20 needles, depending on the weight of the fabric. A cotton-wrapped polyester thread is your best choice. Never mark with wax.

Brocade

The simple definition: A jacquard-weave fabric, usually with a floral pattern. The design

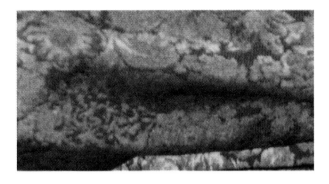

is woven in cotton, silk, wool, or synthetic fiber combinations. Because of the contrast of surfaces in the weave or the contrasting colors, the design appears to be raised. You can find brocade in mid- to heavyweight. Brocatelle, heavier than brocade, is often used for draperies. Brocade makes beautiful draperies and valances in a formal setting such as a living room or master suite.

Care tips: Dry clean and spot clean as needed.

Sewing tips: Use size 70/10 to 90/14 needles. Loosen the machine tension and use long-staple polyester thread. Avoid using wax to mark. If the design is large enough, match it horizontally. Use the nap layout.

Lace

The simple definition: An openwork fabric consisting of a network of threads. Lace can be fragile, but it is also very forgiving. If you make a mistake, it can be hidden. There are hundreds of types of laces includ-

ing Alencon (a solid design outlined with cord on a sheer net background), Battenberg (made of linen braid or tape and linen thread brought together in different designs), Bobbin (handmade, results in an untied lace mesh.), Breton (net with an embroidered design and heavy threads), Brussels (net lace with embroidered designs), Chantilly (bobbin lace with designs outlined by thick, silky threads), and Venetian (a variety of laces that include cutwork, drawn work, and raised point).

Lace works well for double pocket sheers, for French doors, or a simple valance. Lace lined with sheer voile makes beautiful balloon shades in a nursery. Lining the lace helps stabilize it for use in a variety of window treatments.

Care tips: A few laces can be machine washed and dried, but most require dry cleaning. I would vote to do the latter.

Sewing tips: Use size 60/8 to 80/10 needles and extra-fine long-staple polyester thread. Reduce the tension on your machine. Cut with sharp scissors and use the nap layout.

Tapestry

The simple definition: A heavy woven fabric with pictorial or floral design. Because of the pictorial patterns, this fabric is typically used for wall hangings on a rod. Because tapestry is stiff and heavy, with a rough surface, it works well for drapes.

Care tip: Dry clean only.

Sewing tips: Match decorative designs horizontally. Use size 70/10 to 90/14 needles. Lengthen the stitch length and use long-staple polyester thread. Because the fabric can mark easily, use very fine pins.

Calico

The simple definition: A lightweight, plain-weave fabric that usually has a small print design. Calico can tear easily and has a tendency to fray.

Use calico for kitchen café curtains or simple valances. Calico prints also look great in a child's room.

Care tips: Press with a hot iron and plenty of steam. Wash and dry the fabric before cutting.

Sewing tips: Use size 60/8 to 80/12 needles and long-staple polyester thread. Most seam finishes can be used. Check for flaws when buying this fabric.

Acetate

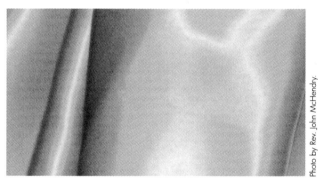

Photo by Rev. John McHendry.

The simple definition: A fabric made from regenerated cellulose fibers, introduced in 1924. This was the first fabric that would melt under the iron. This great fabric drapes beautifully and tends to be resistant to sunlight. Acetate dries quickly. Acetate is used to make a wide range of fabrics such as brocade, lace, and taffeta. Refer to those fabrics for suggestions of which window treatments would be appropriate.

Care tip: Can be laundered or dry cleaned.

Sewing tips: Use a needle size appropriate to the weight of the fabric and long-staple polyester thread.

Fabrics are often categorized to help determine your style and the effect you desire when decorating your windows.

Trellis vines with coordinating chintz print fabric and wallpaper create a garden kitchen.

Cotton chintz prints create a beautiful English Country bedroom.

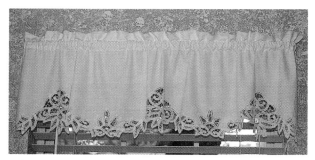

A lace cutwork valance adds a feminine touch.

Velvet and toile tapestry bring to mind a French Country retreat.

Moiré taffeta swags with panels and lace sheers lend a formal touch to this bedroom.

The cotton blend floral fabric used in the valance gives this antique store an English cottage look. The soft hand of the cotton allows the gathers to drape beautifully.

Linen floral pinch-pleated drapes bring a softness to a dark wood-paneled room.

A wide topper with a shaped valance makes this a great corner to curl up and read a good book. The polished cotton creates a formal country look.

Tropical rayon florals accented with animal prints give an air of jungle sophistication.

Simple draperies are all that are needed to frame a beautiful garden view (at least Spot thinks so). This checkered cotton creates a French country atmosphere.

We live in a world full of color. Each day as we look out our window, we see nature's vibrant colors – blue sky, green grass, brightly colored flowers, white snow on the mountain, brown trees, gorgeous birds in flight, and red/yellow sunsets. The reason we go to the beach and watch a sunset is because of the magnificent colors that flash before our eyes. When we decorate a room, we try to bring the outside in. Color does not just involve the fabrics. When you make a change in the window treatment you will often consider changing the color of the walls or the overall color scheme in the room.

Neutral Colors

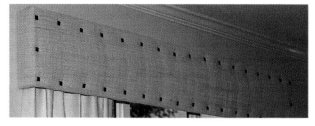

I personally thought a room with only neutral colors would be boring and drab until I was invited to a friend's house for dinner and her whole house was done in neutral tones. I discovered that neutral does not just mean white and off-white – it can be anything from white to black, cream, beige, or brown. My friend's home is light and airy, comfortable, and a feeling of total peace pervades every room. If I ever have the chance to start all over again, I will go with neutrals. Perhaps this is not for everyone, but at least give it a thought.

Shades of Color

Pink is not just pink. There are dark pinks, hot pinks, light pinks, rose pinks, and many more pinks. Shades run the full gamut from light to dark. If you choose only dark shades, the room may appear gloomy and dark. If you choose only light shades, it will be boring at best. It is the combination of shades that produce a balanced look.

By simply changing the window treatment, you can create a whole new color flow throughout the room.

Bold Colors

Bold colors allow you to make a powerful statement and to show off your personality. Creating your own window treatment provides the perfect opportunity to do just that. If you choose a bold fabric, be sure to work with a very large piece on a large window. A 2" x 2" sample will not work.

To add balance, choose one of the strong colors in the fabric and use it throughout the room.

Bold prints come in all different sizes and shapes. Examples of bold fabrics are vivid stripes, colorful plaids, Western prints, and Indian cottons.

Subtle Colors

Perhaps you aren't the "bold" type.

Window treatments can also be subtle. This is a way to create a feeling of elegance in your home. Subtle colors help reduce tension, and who doesn't need that? Actually, incorporating subtle colors can be more difficult than decorating with bold colors. When you use a combination of subtle colors, you need to plan carefully. Think about combinations of colors – plain cream, a cream with a small design, and a variation of cream such as light brown. This will allow the windows to blend in with the walls. When using primarily subtle colors, you might want to insert one accent color.

Examples of subtle fabrics are cotton ticking, sheers, woolen tweeds, and small motifs.

Cool Colors

Being surrounded by cool colors has been proven to slow down the body's metabolism. These colors are often used in hospitals. When using cool colors be careful not to make the room depressing. When I think of cool colors, I think of water. I love movies that are set in Alaska because the beautiful scenery gives me a feeling of peace. Keep in mind that the light coming in the window will affect the fabric you choose.

Examples of cool colors are shades of green to violet, blue, and all shades of gray. Examples of cool fabrics are crisp cottons, soft velvets, cotton checks, poplins, and printed silks.

Warm Colors

Warm colors tend to excite your emotions. This is great in a work area because it can motivate you, but is probably not a good choice in a baby's room. If you are aggressive you will most likely love warm colors. All the shades from red to yellow, including orange, pine, brown, and burgundy, are considered warm.

Examples of warm fabrics are paisley printed cottons, woven ribbed cottons, shades of gold on woven brocades, and damasks.

Prints

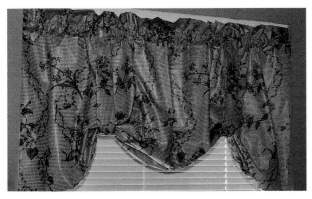

The beauty of printed fabric is the textural quality it adds. It is important to create a balance when using printed fabrics. Use large prints on large windows and small prints on smaller windows. Combine print fabrics with plain fabrics and, if you use a large print, create a small heading.

Examples of printed fabrics are patterned chintzes, cotton motifs, and French toiles.

Sheer and Light Fabrics

Picture in your mind a beautiful puffy cloud. Light fabrics, no matter what color, give you a look of softness or help create a light and airy atmosphere. Light fabrics allow the light to filter into the room, but also give you some degree of privacy.

If using a lace panel, be sure to eliminate any gathers. Lace looks best hung straight on a rod. Light fabrics can also be used in combination with heavier curtains or shades.

Examples of light fabrics are cotton floral prints, laces, small cotton stripes, and muslins.

Heavyweight Fabrics

When using heavy fabrics, you will achieve a room that looks expensive and formal. These are often used in bedrooms because heavier fabrics keep out light. What could be more desirable than a room filled with fabrics that make you feel safe and cozy? Because of the weight of these fabrics, be careful not to use them for tightly pleated drapes. A looser pleat would work well.

Examples of heavy fabrics are silk damasks, brocades, corduroys, tapestries, and reversible fabrics.

Color/Fabric Effect

Color/Fabric	Effect
White	Peacefulness, innocence, and purity
Black	Elegance, wealth
Brown	Richness, rustic, natural
Purple	Royalty, sophistication
Green	Tranquility, outdoors
Blue	Calm, sporty, young
Yellow	Happy, spring-like, sunshine, cheerful
Red	Aristocratic, passionate, romantic
Dark Colors	Intimate
Light Colors	Open and airy
Horizontal Stripes	Make the room seem wider
Vertical Stripes	Make the room seem more spacious (For years women have worn vertical stripes to appear thinner)
Small Prints	Make the room appear larger
Large Prints	Make the room appear smaller
Floral Prints	Large floral prints can be overpowering; small floral prints can give a room a fresh, delicate look
Checked Prints	Subtle checks give the room a country or traditional look; bold checks create a modern look
Ethnic Prints	Ethnic prints are rich with color; from tie-dye to batik, they create a definite mood – use sparingly
Theme Prints	Theme prints are always fun in a child's or baby's room, but we often ignore them when decorating the main rooms of the house. There is no need to do that. Theme prints can quickly give a room a fresh look. For example, a fruit print in the kitchen, a jungle print in a boy's room or den, an animal print in a bathroom.

There is a noticeable difference between an unlined pair of slacks and a lined pair. The lined ones hang better and tend to be warmer. They are also more expensive and are generally of good quality. Adding lining to draperies has the same effect. Because of the lining, the pleats tend to be much fuller and the lining protects the drapery fabric against water stains that can occur from condensation on the window.

The most popular lining fabric is cotton or a cotton/polyester blend. Pure cotton sateen is the number one choice because it comes in many colors, is tightly woven, and won't fade when exposed to light. Let me clarify that statement. It won't fade as much or as quickly as other fabrics. There is no such thing as a 100% colorfast material or dye.

If you want the lining to block all light, use insulating and blackout linings. These are laminated with vinyl or layered with foam acrylic. Interlining also needs to be a consideration because it makes the pleats hang better. This soft flannel material will also provide extra insulation, keeping your home cooler in the summer and warmer in the winter. Buy the lining at the same time you buy the fabric. Check the care labels to make sure you can launder both fabrics together.

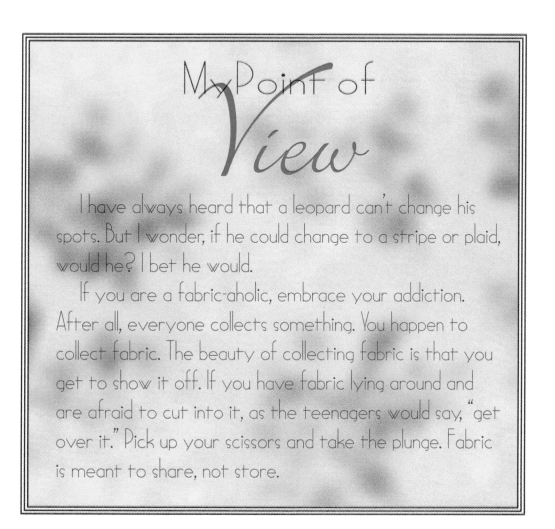

My Point of View

I have always heard that a leopard can't change his spots. But I wonder, if he could change to a stripe or plaid, would he? I bet he would.

If you are a fabric-aholic, embrace your addiction. After all, everyone collects something. You happen to collect fabric. The beauty of collecting fabric is that you get to show it off. If you have fabric lying around and are afraid to cut into it, as the teenagers would say, "get over it." Pick up your scissors and take the plunge. Fabric is meant to share, not store.

View 6

Supplies & Hardware

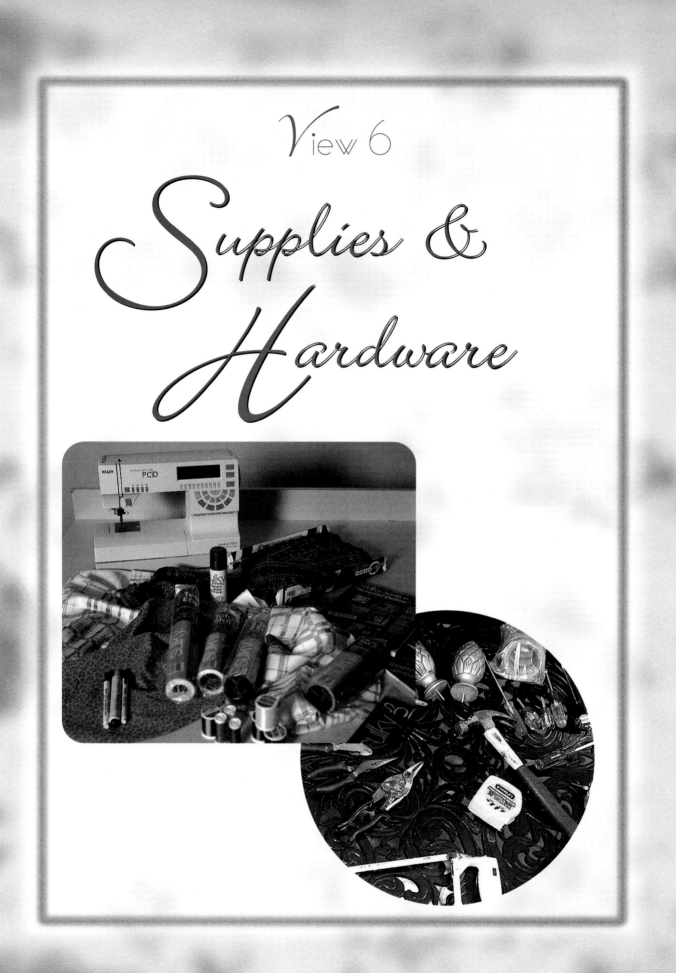

ot everyone can have a traveling workshop like Dal Shirah does. When Dal shows up to install a window treatment, everyone (especially the men) comment, "This is every client's dream." When he opens his giant tool chest, you can see the extension cords, drawers full of nails, screws, and brackets.

Of course, you won't need everything Dal carries with him. Your supply list depends on the window treatment you are installing. Here is an overview of what you might need.

Sewing Machine

Selecting a sewing machine is a very personal decision. I would be foolish to suggest that I know which machine would be best for you. The sewing machines pictured are my personal favorites along with the Babylock Esante' (not pictured). Sewing machines have the ability to stitch many types of stitches that work well when making window treatments. The typical utility stitches include the basting stitch, zigzag stitch, blindstitch, overlock stitch, closed overlock stitch, and more.

Naturally, a sewing machine is most important. When selecting a machine, be sure to try it out before you buy it. To stitch window treatments you need only the basic stitches, so most machines work well, including older machines. But I have to admit, the newer machines take away the frustrations of improper thread tension, broken needles, and stitch selection. Today's machines come with all the necessary feet needed to complete your project.

A serger is a wonderful complement to your sewing machine. Because window treatments require a lot of straight stitching and over edging, a serger makes your work go much faster. Using a two-thread, three-thread, four-thread and more, you can stitch, trim, and finish the seam all in one operation. A serger also allows you to stitch a sturdy, nearly invisible blindhem.

Dal Shirah, a professional installer, has everything he needs in his truck.

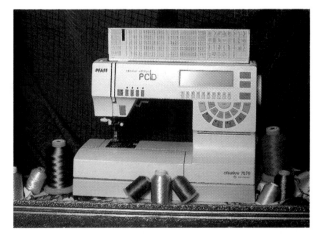

The Pfaff Special Edition PCD with Robinson-Anton threads.

The Viking Designer 1 with Superior threads.

Supplies You May Need

Angle brackets	Level	Screws
Calculator	L-square	Seam gauge
Cleats	Marking pens/pencils	Seam ripper
Craft knife	Molly bolts	Staple gun
Curtain hooks	Needles for hand sewing	Tacks
Curtain weights	Pins	Tailor's chalk
Dowel rods	Plastic rings	Thread, a variety of types
Electric drill	Pleater tape	Toggles
Fiberfill, synthetic	Ruler, metal	T-square
Foam rubber	Scallop template	Velcro
Hammer	Scissors/clippers	Wood glue
Hooks	Screw eyes	Tape measures, dressmaker's and metal
Iron	Screwdriver	

Supplies needed to install window treatments include a tape measure, electric drill, pliers, a hammer, and brackets.

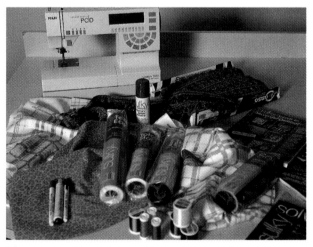

Of course, you'll need a sewing machine and thread. Shown is the Pfaff Special Edition PCD machine with Robinson-Anton threads, Superior threads, and Sulky materials.

By using a pole set, even a simple piece of fabric can look elegant.

Sheer fabrics can be easily clipped onto a spear set and rings. Little or no sewing is required.

Thread a piece of brocade fabric through a floral sconce and you have instant elegance.

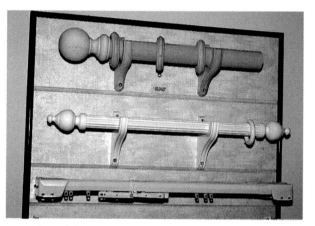

Just a few of the mounting systems available: a wooden dowel, an aluminum rod, and tracks with a built-in pull cord.

The drapes might be finished, but you are not done yet. Your choice of rods, rings, and finials is just as important as the fabric you chose. Through the years these items have been rather standard, but now there are new finishes, new materials, and many new designs. The finishes have gone upscale. You can choose bronze, mahogany, pewter, and others, and you can easily coordinate poles, rods, rings, and finials.

Sconces and finials are both decorative and functional. You can use them with scarves, poles, or a combination of both to achieve a unique and personal fashion statement.

The size rod or pole you purchase will be determined by the size of the rod pocket in your drape (or vice versa, if you are sewing drapes to fit a certain rod). The rod pockets must be large enough to accommodate the rod.

It is easy to underestimate how wide the pocket must be and the "take-up" factor. The circumference of large rods will cause the curtain to hang shorter than the finished length. Therefore, you will need to add for rod take-up. For example, a 1-3/8" round rod requires a 2-1/2" rod pocket and would take-up 1". It would be easy to be fooled into thinking it

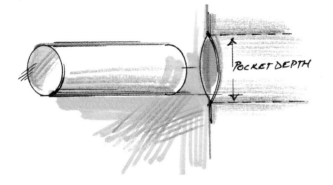

POCKET DEPTH

would require a 1-3/8" pocket. The fabric actually fills some of the room in the pocket. The following chart takes the guesswork out of matching the rod pocket to the rod size and the amount of take-up.

If you are using interlining or a very thick fabric, add 1/2" to the pocket size. If you are using lining, cut it 4" shorter than you cut the curtain fabric. If you are using interlining, cut it 8" shorter than you cut the curtain fabric. These are great rules to follow.

Positioning the Rod/Pole

Selecting the proper drapery hardware is as important as choosing the right fabric for your curtains. The hardware should be determined before measuring the windows for the fabric to assure the treatments will fit properly.

Determine where you want to place the rod above the window. It can be placed just above the window or all the way to ceiling, depending on your window. The rod width should extend beyond the window frame, again depending on how much room you have.

Refer to the rod pocket chart for the appropriate amount of take-up to be added to your final length.

Allow extra length if you want the curtains to break or puddle on the floor. Anywhere from 4" to 18" depending on the look you want to achieve. Remember, part of the fun of creating window treatments is incorporating your own originality.

Type of Rods	Size of Pocket	Take-Up
3/8" solid rod	1"	no take-up
3/4" rod	1-1/2"	1/4"
5/8" pole	1-1/2"	1/2"
1-3/8" pole	2-1/2"	1"
2" pole	4"	1-1/2"
2-1/2"	4-1/2"	1-1/2"
3" pole	5-1/2"	2"

The inspiration.

A Photographic Journey of a Window Treatment in the Making

Enjoy this photo journey through the eyes of a professional installer (Dal Shirah assisted by Dave Polscer). This particular window treatment illustrates a circumstance when you should call for professional assistance. Designer Barbara Hoover, along with homeowners John and Paula Usry, gave window treatment fabricator Robin McCallister an illustration from the 1800s. This was the inspiration for the finished treatment depicted here. After discussions about what they were trying to achieve, such as where rods were to be placed and proper scale, the finished specifications were given to Robin and she took it from there. As you can see, the results are impressive.

Moving the rod up to hang the sheer underlayer.

The sheers in place.

Installing brackets to hold the rods for the main drapes.

Checking the placement for the cornice.

Sliding the drapes onto the rod.

Installing the drapery panels.

Installing the valance.

The drapes and sheers in place.

Checking to make sure the cornice is centered.

Installing the brackets for the valance and cornice.

The tiebacks in place.

The finished window treatment.

With furniture in place.

The window treatment on this page was professionally installed. I sat on the floor with my legs crossed and watched every move the installers made. Photographs were being taken throughout the whole process. It was fascinating to watch. I recommend calling a professional if tackling something this elaborate. It will be well worth the extra money. Obviously, if you were hanging a simple rod, this wouldn't be necessary. If you have spent a lot of time and energy making a window treatment, you certainly want to see it hung properly.

View 7

"Pane"-less Techniques

Because a window is often the focal point in a room, it is important that you pay close attention to proportions. Most of the time a window is half as wide as it is high. Obviously this is not always true, so pay close attention to accurate measuring.

It is best to mount your hardware first so you will get more accurate measurements. Use a metal tape measure and measure each window separately. Windows may look exactly alike, but they can vary enough to make a difference. Don't take the chance. Half the battle of making your own window treatments is getting the correct measurements.

By taking all these measurements, you will be secure in knowing you have everything you need. Make a copy of this illustration and insert the measurements of your window. This will help you decide where to place the rods, how long you want the panels, etc. Take the copy with you when you go to buy the fabric and hardware. You may end up with more measurements than you need, but more information is much better than not enough.

1. Measure the width of the window from casing to casing.

2. Measure the length of the window from the top of the casing to the top of the sill.

3. Measure from the top of the window to the bottom of the sill.

4. Measure from the top of the window to the floor.

5. Measure the inside of the window from the sash to the top of the sill.

6. Measure the inside of the window from jamb to jamb.

7. Measure the lower portion of the window from the top of the lower sash (if there is one) to the top of the sill.

8. Measure from the top of the window to the ceiling.

9. Measure the wall area from outside the left casing to any obstruction (such as another window or radiator).

10. Measure the wall area from the outside of the right casing for any obstruction.

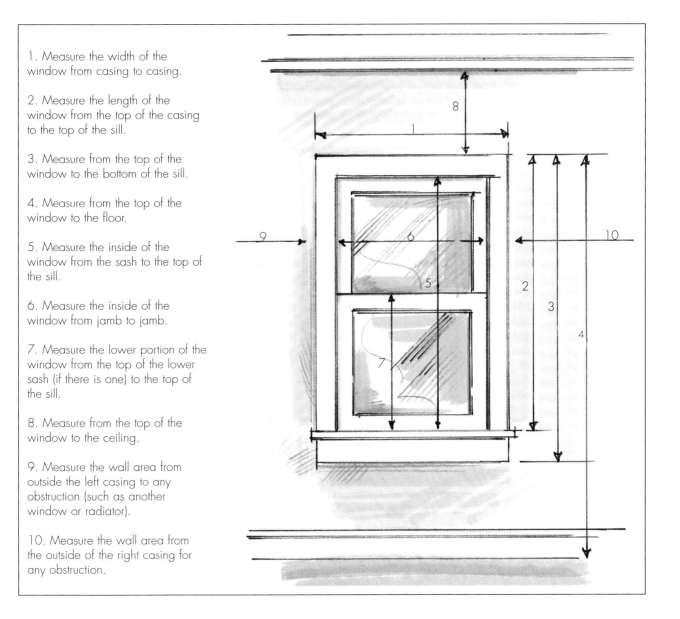

Measure for Finished Length

1. Measure from the top of the rod or heading to the desired length (sill, apron, floor, or puddled).

2. Add hem allowances, casing measurements, heading, and pattern repeats if applicable. This is what is referred to as the **finished cutting length**.

* If using a casing but no heading, add 1/2" to the diameter of the rod for turning under and another 1/4" to 1" (depending on the thickness of the fabric) for ease in handling. Refer to the rod pocket size chart on page 50.
* For the bottom hems, add double the desired hem to the finished length. For sheer or lightweight fabrics, allow for a 5" to 6" double hem by adding 10" to 12" to the length. For medium weight fabrics, allow for a 4" double hem by adding 8" to the length. If making short curtains or a valance, allow for a 1" to 3" double hem by adding 2" to 6" to the length.
* If your fabric has a pattern repeat, measure the distance between motifs and add one repeat per cutting length.

Measure for Finished Width

1. Measure the rod width and add the two returns.

* Adjust for the desired fullness. This will depend on the weight of the fabric. For medium to heavyweight fabrics, add 2 to 2-1/2 times the finished width. For sheer and lightweight fabrics, add 2-1/2 to 3 times the finished width.
* If the panels are not wider than the fabric, you don't need to add any extra for seam allowances. If there are multi-panels, add 1" for each seam.
* Add 4" per panel for side hems. This results in a 1" double-fold hem on each side of the panel.
* If the curtains are going to overlap, add extra.

Calculate Yardage for Fabric Without a Pattern Repeat

Finished length   _____
Add bottom hem doubled   +_____
Add casing and headings   +_____
Total   =_____
                (cutting length of fabric)

Finished width   _____
Multiply width by fullness   x_____
     factor (2-1/2 or 3)   =_____
Add side hems   +_____
Add seams as applicable   +_____

Total   =_____
                (cutting width of fabric)

Calculate Yardage for Fabric With a Pattern Repeat

The length doesn't change.

Distance between pattern repeats   _____
Multiply by finished width   x_____
                    =_____
                (cutting width of fabric)

There is no set amount of fabric you will need for a particular window treatment. All windows are different and fabrics vary by repeat and width. You must consider the type of heading, fabric repeats, and of course, the style. For instance, if you create a 4" heading instead of a 2" heading, you will obviously need more fabric.

How to Allow for Rod Take-Up

It's easy to measure the length of a curtain while the fabric is lying on the table, but if you do that, the curtain will come up short. Why?

Because when the fabric is pushed onto the rod, it causes the length to shorten. See the rod pocket size chart on page 50 to determine how much fabric to add for take-up.

Before pinning and stitching the final bottom hem, it's a good idea to let the curtains hang for a day or two.

* Check and double-check the exact location of the rod.
* Curtains with a header will draw up more than those without a header.
* A round rod draws the curtain up more than a flat rod.
* A lined drape will draw up more than an unlined drape or one made from sheer fabric.
* The more fabric you push onto a rod, the more it will draw up.
* A tight pocket on a rod will tend to draw up more than a loose pocket.

Cutting and Matching

Cutting the fabric and matching a pattern is just as important as the actual sewing. You need to prepare the "palette."

The fabric must be cut on the true lengthwise and crosswise grain to hang straight. The best way to do this is to pull a thread on the crosswise grain and then cut along that thread. Another method is to use a carpenter's square. Place one side of the square on the selvage edge, then mark along the other side of the square. Cut on that line. If there is a pattern, you can cut along that pattern. Whichever method you use, be sure to be accurate.

When your fabric has a pattern, you need to buy extra fabric to match the design. If you are using decorator fabrics you will find the designs are split evenly at the selvage. This makes it simple to match. To align the designs you can use fusible web or pins to hold the seam in place before sewing the seam.

A word about matching. No matter how careful you are when pinning the seam, the material shifts when you sew it so that after you have sewn the seam you will find the pattern off by about 1/8". Here's how to keep that from happening. When sewing a seam there are two pieces of fabric – the top piece that goes directly under the sewing machine foot, and the bottom piece that is under that piece but touching the feed dog. Align the pattern you are matching so the top piece is 1/8" behind the bottom piece. When you sew the seam, the sewing machine foot will move the top piece forward 1/8" and the pattern will be lined up exactly. Once you get used to this technique you will never do it any other way.

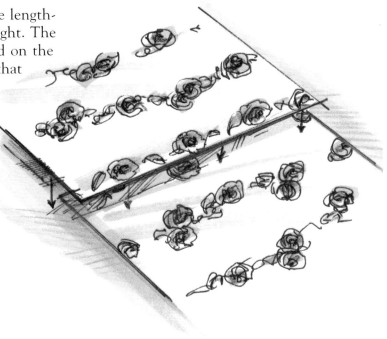

A double fold hem is often used when making window treatments. Double fold means exactly that – you fold up the fabric the hem width, then fold it up again. A double fold hem is also used on the side hems.

Simply turn up the hem width two times to the wrong side of the fabric and pin and press. Straight stitch the hem edge, using 8 to 10 stitches per inch. For heavyweight fabric, lessen the tension slightly and stitch slowly. Alternatively, you can use a machine blind-stitch or fusible web.

A Perfect Hem Corner

1. Measure 3" up on each side of the corner. Measure another 3". Press the 3" folds.

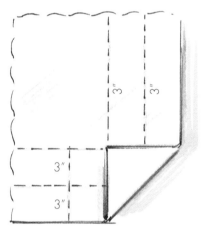

2. Open the folds and fold the corner diagonally as illustrated.

3. Fold the corner diagonally again.

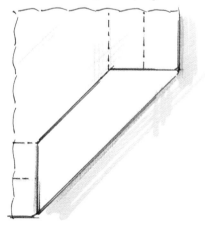

4. Open out the corner and with right sides together, pin on the diagonal fold line. Stitch on the fold line at a right angle to the corner fold.

5. Trim off the excess point and turn the corner to the right side.

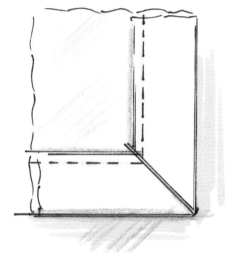

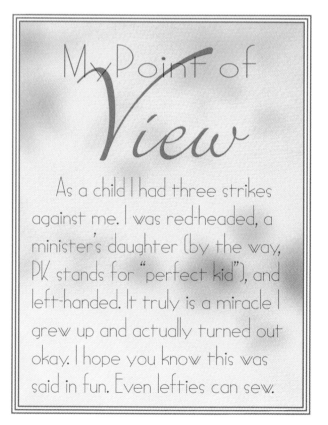

6. Press the corner and stitch the hem.

My Point of
View

As a child I had three strikes against me. I was red-headed, a minister's daughter (by the way, PK stands for "perfect kid"), and left-handed. It truly is a miracle I grew up and actually turned out okay. I hope you know this was said in fun. Even lefties can sew.

View 8

Valances & Cornices

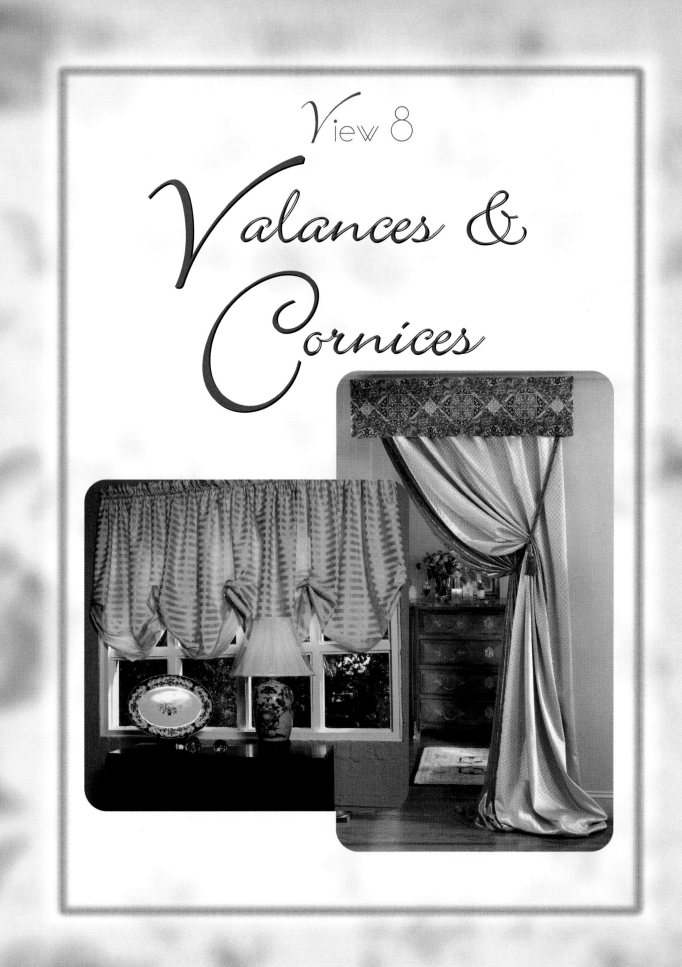

*L*et's take a quick look at the dictionary definitions for valance and cornice. I believe it is interesting to note the etymology and function of these words. From *Webster's International Dictionary*.

When you see the words valance and cornice in such a cold context, it is hard to believe that they can add such charm to a room. Both are decorative headings that are placed above curtains, shades, and draperies and add a finished look to the top of the window. They can also add height, help disguise challenging windows, or hide rods and mountings.

va·lance

Function: noun

Etymology: Middle English vallance, perhaps from Valence, France

Date: 15th century
1. A drapery hung along the edge of a bed, table, altar, canopy, or shelf.
2. A short drapery, or wood or metal frame, used as a decorative heading to conceal the top of curtains and fixtures.

cor·nice

Function: noun
Etymology: Middle French, from Italian frame, cornice, from Latin cornic-, cornix crow; akin to Greek korax raven
Date: 1563

1. a. The molded and projecting horizontal member that crowns an architectural composition, b. the top course that crowns a wall.
2. A decorative band of metal or wood used to conceal curtain fixtures.

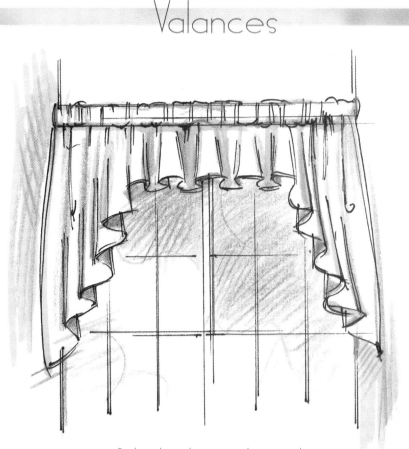

Rod pocket valances can be tapered.

A valance is a fabric heading. It can be shirred, flat, trimmed, plain, pleated, or shaped. A valance is hung from a rod, pole, or board. A shirred valance is a short gathered panel that extends 1" to 2" in front of a curtain rod. Extra fabric is pushed together to give it fullness. A flat (or tailored) valance has no extra fullness. The standard length of a valance is typically 12" to 18" or 1/5 the length of the entire window treatment.

The **rod pocket valance** is definitely the most popular. These are often tapered, scalloped, arched, or shaped. The easiest to make is a simple no-nonsense rod pocket valance (see page 63 for instructions).

Banner or handkerchief valances are hung from a rod or mounted on a board. These are flat panels with pointed or shaped lower edges. They are sometimes accented with cording, banding, or tassels. See page 79 for making instructions.

The most common type of valance is the rod pocket valance.

Banner valances are easy to make and allow a good view of the outdoors.

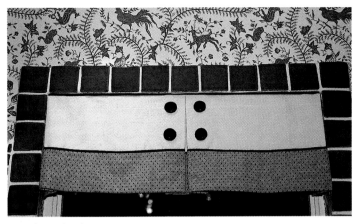

Box-pleated valance.

Box-pleated valances give your room a tailored look. They are great for a den or office. The box pleats have equally spaced inverted pleats and can be accented with a contrasting band or welting, or contrasting inserted pleats and buttons. See page 75 for making instructions.

Balloon valances are usually stationary and the poufs or scallops along the lower edge are permanent. These look great in bedrooms and certainly dress up a kitchen. They can also be done as a working shade that eliminates the need for mini-blinds. The working balloon shade fulfills the need for privacy. See page 69 for making instructions.

Self-valances are another favorite. You often see these on shower curtains. These valances are sewn into the heading of the curtain panel instead of being hung separately.

A stationary balloon valance with a rod pocket and heading.

Self-valances are sewn into the heading of the curtain panel.

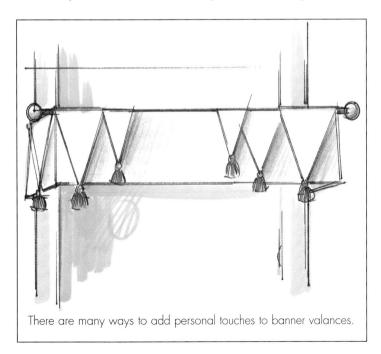

There are many ways to add personal touches to banner valances.

How to Make a Lined Rod Pocket Valance

heading

rod pocket

For the valance shown in the photo, the 40" x 1" rod extends 2" beyond each side of the window and has a 2-1/2" return. The 18" long valance is hung 6" above the window. These instructions will give you a 2-1/2" header and a 1-1/2" rod pocket. These measurements are just for illustrative purposes - your measurements will likely be different.

You Will Need

* Curtain rod and appropriate hardware
* Decorator fabric (see below to calculate yardage)
* Lining fabric (same amount)

Directions

1. To determine **how many fabric widths** you need:

	Example
Measure the rod width	40"
Add 2 returns (2 x 2-1/2")	+ 5"
	45"
Multiply by 2-1/2 times fullness	x 2-1/2
	112-1/2"
Divide by fabric width & round up (most decorator fabrics are 54" wide)	÷ 54"
	2.08

You will need **2 widths of fabric**. Be sure to purchase extra fabric to accommodate a pattern repeat if applicable. Pattern repeat occurs when there is an obvious repeat of a motif. To determine the extra amount of fabric needed, measure the distance between repeats. Multiply this distance by the number of panels. That will tell you how much to buy.

2. To determine **how long** to cut the fabric:

	Example
Start with the finished length	18"
Add twice the rod pocket (2 x 1-1/2")	+ 3"
Add twice the header (2 x 2-1/2")	+ 5"
Add 1/2" seam allowance	+ 1/2"
	26-1/2"

Cut the fabric 26-1/2" long.

3. To determine the **total yardage** required:

	Example
Start with the number of widths (from Step 1)	2
Multiply times the cut length (from Step 2)	x 26-1/2"
	53"
Divide by 36 & round up	÷ 36
	1.47

You will need a total of 1-1/2 yards of fabric.

4. Cutting the fabric: Cut each of the 2 widths 26-1/2" long.

5. Sewing the valance: With right sides together and using a 1/2" seam allowance, sew the widths together, making sure to match the print where the seams will be. This will produce a single piece of fabric 112-1/2" wide x 26-1/2" long. To avoid seams at the center, cut one of the 26-1/2" lengths in half between the selvages and sew half to each side of the center piece.

6. Repeat Step 5 with the lining fabric.

7. With right sides together and using a 1/2" seam allowance, stitch the decorative fabric to the lining fabric along the two sides and bottom, leaving the top open.

8. Trim the seams and corners and turn right side out. Press.

9. Serge or zigzag stitch the top edge.

10. On the top edge, press down 4", which is the amount of the rod pocket + the header (1-1/2" + 2-1/2"). Press down another 4". This creates a double folded rod pocket and header.

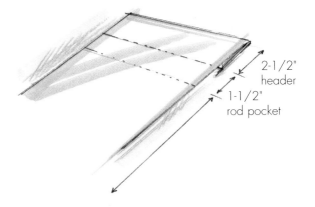

2-1/2" header

1-1/2" rod pocket

11. To create the rod pocket, stitch two lines – one near the pressed edge and one 1-1/2" below.

12. Insert the rod or dowel in the pocket.

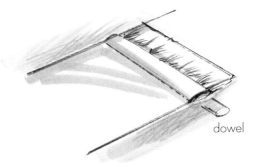

dowel

Inspirational Potpourri

This rod pocket valance was pulled up with contrasting bows.

To change the look of a rod pocket valance, try adding a contrasting ruffle and shaping the bottom edge. This mock balloon look is achieved by drawing up the valance in two places. Cut a strip of contrasting fabric twice the length of the bottom edge, fold it in half to the wrong side, ruffle, and stitch it to the lower edge.

Even the simplest rod pocket valance can be enhanced with a contrasting lining and shaped edges. Simply self-line and shape the bottom edge to your liking.

A contrasting centerpiece and appliqué adds drama to this rod pocket valance. Use a contrasting fabric in the center of the treatment. Cut out a flower from the print and appliqué it in the center. Looks hard to do, but is so simple.

A shaped, rod pocket valance. This one-piece valance looks just like a valance with tails.

A simple rod pocket valance with a banded bottom edge. To add the band, cut a strip of fabric the same length as the bottom edge of the valance and twice as wide as you want the band to be plus hem allowance. Hem the raw edges and fold the band to encompass the bottom edge of the valance. Stitch in place.

This valance is basically the same as a rod pocket valance except it has been hand gathered and stapled to a shaped board with a rope accent. You can see what a nice effect this has.

Instead of making a rod pocket, you can hang a valance on a rod with sewn-in rings.
The pattern for this valance is from Southern Living.

Yet another way to skip the rod pocket and hang a valance. This pattern is the Southern Living Celebration Valance.

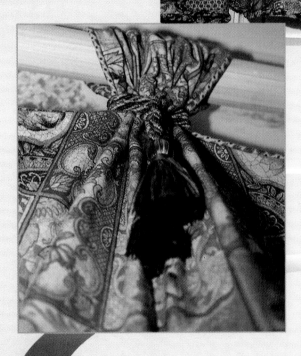

By using the finished edge of some laces, you can just stitch in a rod pocket and hang. This allows the light to come in.

When you combine shape and a soft print, you get this lovely valance.

Using a soft striped fabric, you create a casual but elegant window treatment. This balloon valance can be made with or without a ruffle on the bottom edge. Here, the bottom edge is unadorned, but you could easily add a ruffle, braiding, tassels, or any other type of trim that appeals to you.

Balloon valances are often called cloud or pouf valances. The choice of fabric can make a dramatic difference in the look of a valance. For example, a balloon valance with a contrasting ruffle in soft chintz would be perfect in a child's room. The same valance done in silk would be ideal in a more formal setting.

In the example pictured, the finished width is 42" wide with 2" returns and the finished length is 30". The header is 3" and the 1" curtain rod requires a 1-1/2" rod pocket. These measurements are for illustrative purposes only. Your measurements will be different to fit your window.

You Will Need

* 1" curtain rod and appropriate hardware
* Decorator fabric (see below to calculate yardage)
* Lining fabric (same amount)
* 1/2" metal rings
* 1/4" cord
* *Optional:* Nylon netting to stuff poufs

Directions

1. To determine **how many fabric widths** you'll need:

	Example
Measure the width of the rod	42"
Add 2 returns (2 x 2")	+ 4"
Add seam allowance for sides	+ 1"
Multiply by 3 for fullness	x 3
	141"
Divide by fabric width & round up (most decorator fabric is 54" wide)	÷ 54"
	2.61

You will need 3 widths of fabric. Be sure to purchase extra fabric to accommodate a pattern repeat if necessary.

2. To determine the **cut length** of the fabric:

	Example
Start with the finished length	30"
Add 24" for pouf	+ 24"
Add double the rod pocket (2 x 1-1/2")	+ 3"
Add double the header (2 x 3")	+ 6"
	63"

Cut the fabric 63" long.

3. To determine the **total yardage** required:

	Example
Start with the number of widths (from Step 1)	3
Multiply times the cut length (from Step 2)	x 63"
	189"
Divide by 36 & round up	÷ 36
	5.25

You will need a total of 5-1/4 yards of fabric. Be sure to add extra fabric to match pattern repeats if necessary.

4. Cutting the fabric: Cut each of the 3 widths 63" long, being sure to accommodate pattern repeat if applicable.

5. Sewing the valance: With right sides together and using a 1/2" seam allowance, sew the widths together, matching the fabric pattern (if applicable) at the seams. Do the same for the lining.

6. Placing the right side of the fabric and lining together, sew a 1/2" seam around the 2 sides and bottom, leaving the top open. Turn and press the seams.

7. Spread the fabric on a flat surface and fold down the top edge the amount of the header and rod pocket (4-1/2" in this example). Turn down again, creating a double pocket and header.

8. Stitch across the full width of the fabric close to the creased edge.

9. Measure down 3" from the top of the folded fabric and sew across the full width of the fabric. This creates a 3" header and a 1-1/2" rod pocket for the rod.

10. Determine the number and placement of the poufs. On the wrong side of the valance, mark for ring spacing. You will sew on a vertical column of rings for each pouf. Begin the first column 1/2" in from the side seam and mark for a ring every 6" from bottom to top. Make sure the marks line up evenly.

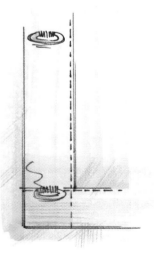

11. Hand stitch one ring at each mark.

12. Thread and tie cords through the columns of rings to draw the valance up the desired amount.

13. Insert the rod into the rod pocket and hang on the installed brackets. Adjust the gathers and knot the four cords together to secure.

14. If necessary, stuff the poufs with nylon netting.

Inspirational Potpourri

A floral balloon valance.

This stationary tailored balloon valance coordinates with the wallpaper.

A striped balloon valance. Eliminating the rings on the side allows the valance to hang down on the side.

A ruffled balloon valance.

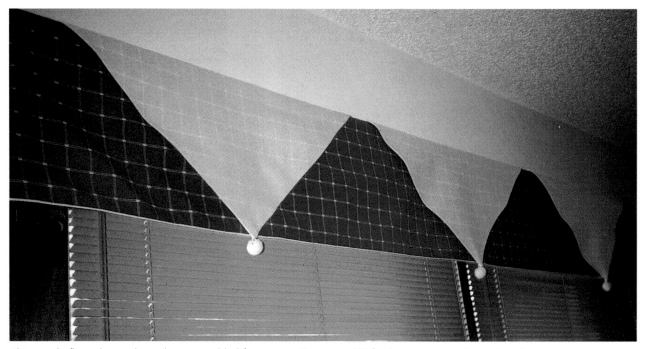

This simple flat valance shows banners added for accent. See page 79 for the instructions for making banners.

Flat valances are also called soft cornices. In this example, the finished width is 72" with 3-1/2" returns and the finished length is 15". These measurements are for illustrative purposes only. Your measurements will be different to fit your window.

You Will Need

* Mounting board
* Appropriate hardware to mount board to wall
* Decorator fabric (see below to calculate yardage)
* Lining fabric (same amount)
* Staple gun or glue

Directions

1. To determine **how many fabric widths** you need:

	Example
Measure the rod width	72"
Add 2 returns (2 x 3-1/2")	+ 7"
Add seam allowance	+ 1"
	80"
Divide by fabric width & round up (most decorator fabric is 54" wide)	÷ 54"
	1.48

You will need 2 fabric widths.

2. To determine **how long** to cut the fabric:

	Example
Start with the finished length	15"
Add 2" for the board	+ 2"
Add 1/2" for bottom seam allowance.	+ 1/2"
	17-1/2"

Cut the fabric 17-1/2" long.

3. To determine the **total yardage** required:

Example

Start with the number of widths
(from Step 1) 2

Multiply times the cut length
(from Step 2) x 17-1/2"

  35"

Divide by 36 & round up ÷ 36
. .97"

You will need 1 yard of fabric. Be sure to allow for pattern repeats if applicable.

4. Cutting the fabric: Cut each of the 2 widths 17-1/2" long. Repeat with the lining fabric.

5. Sewing the valance: With right sides together and using a 1/2" seam allowance, stitch the widths together to form one piece of fabric 108" wide (twice the 54" width) x 17-1/2" long.

To avoid seams at the center, cut one of the 17-1/2" lengths in half between the selvages and sew half to each side of the center piece. You will need to cut off some of the width to have a piece of fabric 80" wide x 17-1/2" long.

6. As in the photo, add contrasting cording to the bottom hem for a decorative effect.

7. With right sides together, stitch the lining and decorator fabrics together on both sides and across the bottom.

8. Turn right side out and press.

9. Serge or zigzag the top edge.

10. Press in returns (3-1/2") on each side.

11. Staple or glue the fabric piece on the mounting board and install the board on the wall.

This flat valance has slight scallops on the bottom edge. The bottom of the valance was cut shaped and a decorative rope was added for accents.

Inspirational Potpourri

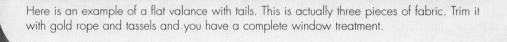

Here is an example of a flat valance with tails. This is actually three pieces of fabric. Trim it with gold rope and tassels and you have a complete window treatment.

This one-rod flat valance has a shaped bottom edge.

The box-pleated valance shown is mounted on a 1" x 4" x 40" wide cornice board with 3-1/2" returns. These measurements are for illustrative purposes. Adjust your measurements to fit your window.

You Will Need

* Mounting board
* Appropriate hardware to mount board on wall
* Decorator fabric (see below to calculate yardage)
* Lining fabric (same amount)
* Decorative braid
* Staple gun or glue

Directions

1. To determine **how many fabric widths** you need:

	Example
Measure the board width	40"
Add 2 returns (2 x 3-1/2")	+ 7"
Add 12" per box pleat (4 x 12")	+ 48"
Add 6" for each corner pleat (2 x 6")	+ 12"
Add 1/2" for each side seam allowance	+ 1"
	108"
Divide by fabric width & round up (most decorator fabric is 54" wide)	÷ 54"
	2

You will need 2 widths of fabric.

2. To determine **how long** to cut the fabric:

	Example
Start with the finished length	18"
Add 2" for the board	+ 2"
Add 1/2" for the bottom seam allowance	+ 1/2"
	20-1/2"

Cut the fabric 20-1/2" long.

3. To determine the **total yardage** required:

	Example
Start with the number of widths (from Step 1)	2
Multiply times the cut length (from Step 2)	x 20-1/2"
	41"
Divide by 36 & round up	÷ 36
	1.13"

You will need 1-1/4 yards of fabric. Purchase extra fabric to accommodate repeats if applicable.

4. Cutting the fabric: Cut each of the 2 widths of the decorator fabric 20-1/2" long. Repeat with the lining fabric.

5. Sewing the valance: With right sides together and using a 1/2" seam allowance, sew the decorator fabric widths together, making sure to match the print where the seams will be. To avoid seams at the center, split one cut between the selvages and sew to each side of the center piece. You should have one piece of fabric 23" long x 108" wide (twice the 54" width). Repeat with the lining fabric.

6. With right sides together and leaving the top edge open, sew a 1/2" seam around the side and along the bottom edge.

7. Turn right side out and press.

8. Serge or zigzag the top edge.

9. Sew the decorative braid along the bottom.

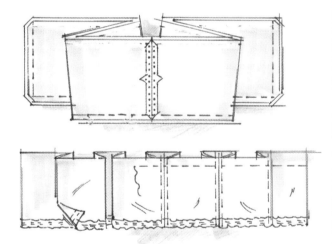

10. By hand, fold the fabric to form pleats so it fits the width of the board or rod plus the returns.

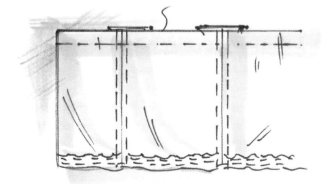

11. Baste the pleats in place across the top. When you are satisfied with the position of the pleats, press them in.

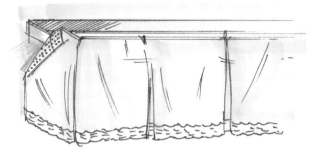

12. Staple or glue the pleated valance to the board. If desired, you can paint or cover the board with fabric before stapling on the valance.

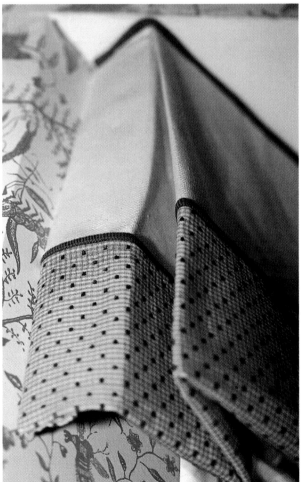

When going around a corner, add a pleat at the corner.

Inspirational Potpourri

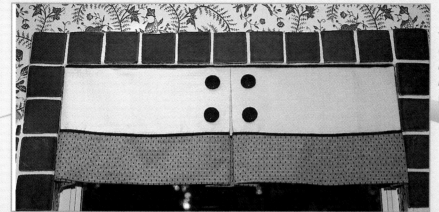

This box-pleated valance over the kitchen sink is made with two different fabrics. Simplicity and McCall's have a vast variety of patterns to choose from.

The same treatment carried over into the dining area.

The center pleat and button accents add interest.

An inverted box pleat made with cotton print fabric.

This box-pleated valance has contrasting insets that are pulled open and stitched.

This super-easy banner valance is made with two contrasting fabrics and a braid trim.

Banner valances are also called handkerchief valances and are really easy to make. They add an element of fun to any room. The fabric requirements will depend on the size of your window and how much of it you want the valance to cover. Make paper patterns first, then calculate the yardage requirements based on the patterns.

You Will Need

* Mounting board
* Appropriate hardware to mount board to wall
* Fabric #1
* Contrasting fabric #2
* Lining fabric
* Craft paper
* Decorative braid trim
* Staple gun or glue

Directions

1. Determine the size of the banner you will need to cover your window. Make two patterns from craft paper – one for the large triangle and one for the smaller triangle overlay. Experiment with the paper patterns before cutting the pieces from fabric. You may have to make a few experimental triangles before you arrive at the right sizes. Hold the paper pieces in place on the window when deciding.

2. Cut triangles from both fabrics and cut the lining fabric the size of the larger triangle.

3. Place the larger fabric triangle on a flat surface and lay the smaller triangle on top of it. This will give the illusion of a contrast banding.

4. Stitch the two fabric pieces together, then stitch braiding to cover the stitching line.

5. Place the fabric and lining right side together and stitch the side and bottom. Stitch down to the point, take one stitch across (and only one) and then stitch up the other side. This one stitch allows you to turn the fabric and make a clean, crisp point.

6. Turn right side out. Stitch or serge the top edge and press.

7. Staple or glue the finished banner on the mounting board and install the board on the wall.

Inspirational Potpourri

This handkerchief valance is accented with tassels and cording around the panels. This design was inspired by an illustration from a Victorian-era drawing. We took the drawing and enlarged it at the copy center to create the shape we wanted.

The graduating size of these tasseled triangle banners makes for an interesting look. The triangles and the flat valance are attached to a top board.

This handkerchief valance covers a stagecoach shade that can be rolled up.

Another idea for adding triangles over a flat valance.

This shaped valance is mounted on a board that covers the top of a stationary curtain.

To use both a valance and stationary curtains, you need two rods or one rod and a mounting board. The instructions that follow are for two rods.

You Will Need

* Valance
* Curtain
* Continental rod
* Standard curtain rod

Directions

1. Mount the standard curtain rod at the upper edge of the window.

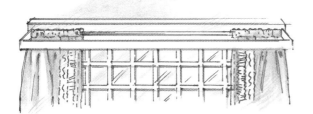

2. Hang the stationary drapery panels on the standard curtain rod.

3. Mount the Continental rod (or mounting board) in front of the standard rod.

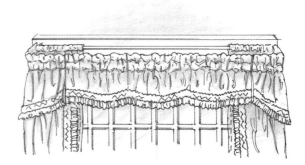

4. Hang the valance on the Continental rod and arrange the gathers evenly.

This valance mounted over curtains and blinds was made from a commercial pattern called the Manhattan Valance. The contrasting center jabot is a great finishing touch.

Inspirational Potpourri

This triangle valance is mounted over a shade and uses grommets and boating rope to create a nautical effect.

This shower curtain and valance, made from a commercial workroom pattern, are mounted on two different shower rods.

This shaped valance is made with two coordinating fabrics. It has a monogram velvet overlay with matching velvet side panels.

This hard cornice has been covered with raffia fabric and accented with upholstery nail heads.

A **cornice or pelmet** is a box-like structure made from wood, foam board, or heavy cardboard. Cornices are usually padded or upholstered. Many have closed tops that protect the curtains from dust. (Too bad we can't create a giant cornice that would cover the whole house!) Besides being decorative, a cornice makes the window more energy efficient because it restricts the airflow at the top. It also stops light from filtering in through the top of the curtain. Cornices don't have to be plain. Here are some unique designs for cornices.

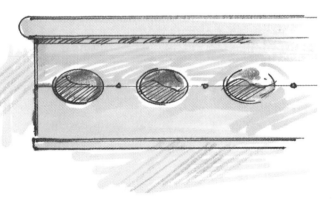

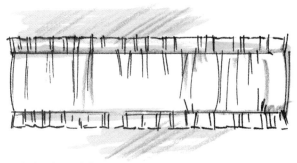

Triple/wide middle.

Cornices are usually 1/6 the curtain or shade length, 3" to 4" wider than the window treatment, and project 2" to 3" in front of it. Because it is screwed in place, a cornice is a semi-permanent fixture that can be removed for cleaning.

If you choose to upholster the cornice, avoid sheer or open weave fabrics and use a firm interfacing such as buckram to prevent the air that seeps in at the top of the window from warping the interfacing. Buckram is an open weave fabric that has been treated to make it stiff. Believe it or not, you can also buy iron-on buckram. When using buckram, back it with bump interlining or use iron-on interfacing. By doing this you create a smooth finish. There are also self-adhesive stiffeners with peel-off backing paper. No lining is necessary when using this. Double-sided stiffener has adhesive on both sides and requires lining, but creates a neater finish.

There is some crossover between valances and cornices. These could both be called headings or toppers.

Velcro works great for attaching a fabric valance to a cornice board. Here's a great idea: Make a reversible valance and attach it with Velcro. That way, if you get tired of the fabric, you can reverse it and get a whole new look.

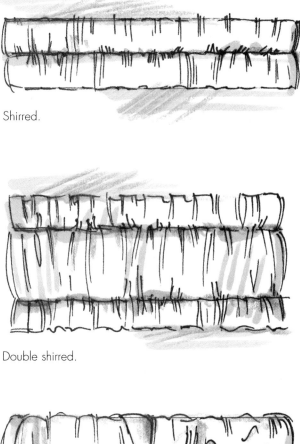

Shirred.

Double shirred.

Triple/wide middle plus wider edges.

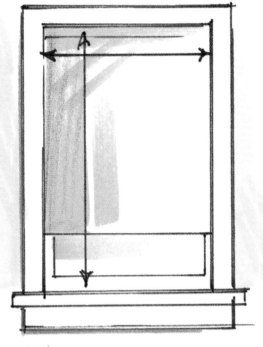

Inside mount.

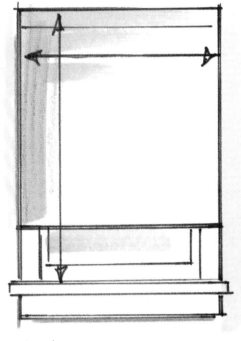

Outside mount.

To mount the cornice **inside** the window frame, the recess must be deep enough to accommodate both the under treatment (curtain, shade, mini blinds, etc.) and the cornice. Allow a minimum of 1/2" (1-1/8" over vertical blinds) between the back of the cornice and the face of the under treatment. Remember that the cornice board thickness influences how far the cornice projects beyond the under treatment.

To mount the cornice **outside** the window frame, determine the inside width of the cornice, and add a minimum of 1/2" to the width of the under treatment. To determine the return depth from the inside edge of the cornice to the wall, allow a minimum of 1/2" (1-1/8" over verticals) between the back of the cornice and the face of the under treatment. Remember that the cornice board thickness influences how far the cornice projects beyond the under treatment on the front and returns.

The cornice generally should not be longer than 1/6 the full length of the curtain, but this is not set in stone. Stand back and see what you think.

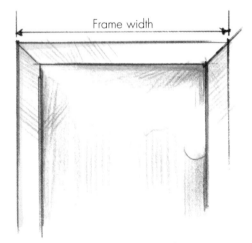

Frame width

To calculate the width of the cornice, for a frame window, measure corner to corner. For a no-frame window, measure the opening and add 4".

2"   Opening plus 4"   2"

How to Install Board-Mounted Treatments

You Will Need

* Complete window treatment
* Complete cornice board
* Angle brackets and screws or toggle bolts
* Staple gun
* Optional: Velcro

For illustrative purposes, the boards are shown with the treatment not attached so you get a better view of what is going on underneath when installing. The cornice board below consists of a top board only, but others are three-sided boxes made of a top, two sides, and a front. Obviously the latter gives more support and should be used for very heavy window treatments.

Directions

1. If desired, paint or cover the board.

2. On the underside of the board, measure and mark the placement of the angle brackets an equal distance in from each end, allowing 1" of

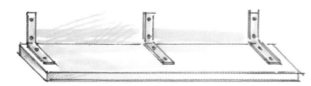

Angle brackets mounted on the underside of the cornice board.

space beyond each side edge of the window frame. For now, mark only, don't attach the brackets to the board.

3. With the cornice board centered over the window at the desired height, mark the angle bracket placements on the wall. Use a level to make sure the board is level.

4. Attach the brackets to the wall with screws or toggle bolts.

5. Position the board on the angle brackets above the window and attach the board to the brackets.

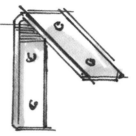

Attach the angle brackets to the wall.

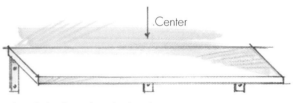

Attach the board to the brackets.

6. Staple the valance to the upper front and side edges of the cornice board. If you don't want to staple through the fabric valance, sew a strip of Velcro to the valance and staple the opposite Velcro strip to the cornice board, then mount the valance with Velcro.

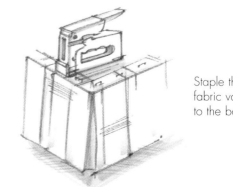

Staple the fabric valance to the board.

Inspirational Potpourri

Here a flat cornice has been combined with draperies for a dramatic effect on a door.

Photo courtesy of Graber (Hand-Carved Wood Ware by Springs Window Fashions), Middleton, Wis.

A soft shaped cornice that has been board mounted. This style uses a small amount of fabric, so you get more bang for your buck.

A soft cornice with angled sides.

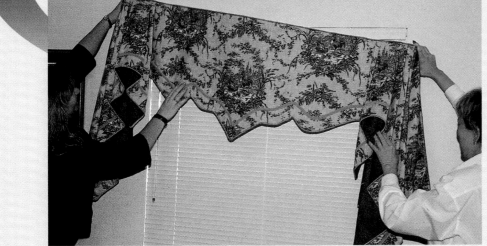

A soft cornice mounted on a shaped board. Note the detail of the contrasting gimp and welt cord.

A wood cornice with wallpaper cutouts. The designer who created this treatment cut out 1/4" plywood the shape of her wallpaper border to create this topper and accented it with cords and tassels.

A mock pleated valance mounted on a board. This is a great way to use up leftover fabric. Just staple the contrasting pieces of fabric to the board for a great look.

A fabric valance with contrasting welt and lining mounted on a cornice board.

My Point of

View

I joined Robin McCallister in her classroom the day she was making a cornice board, so I watched closely. I never dreamed making a cornice was so simple. Consider making one yourself – it really is a simple process.

View 9
Cascades (Jabots) & Swags

ja·bot

Function: noun
Etymology: French
Date: 1823
1. A fall of lace or cloth attached to the front of a neckband and worn especially by men in the 18th century.
2. A pleated frill of cloth or lace attached down the center front of a woman's blouse or dress.

cas·cade

Function: noun
Etymology: French, from Italian cascata, from cascare to fall, from (assumed) Vulgar Latin casicare, from Latin casus fall
Date: 1641
1. A steep, usually small fall of water, especially: one of a series.
2. Something falling or rushing forth in quantity <a cascade of sound> <a cascade of events>.

Does a jabot equal a cascade, or does a cascade equal a jabot? Actually they are the same thing.

swag

Function: noun
Date: 1660
1. Something (as a decoration) hanging in a curve between two points.

During the 19th century a drapery could consist of one, two, or three swags with a single tail (also called a jabot or cascade) at each side. As time went on, the swag became more voluminous. This continuous length of fabric was introduced for the purpose of linking two or more windows on the same wall.

When selecting fabric for swags, make sure the fabric drapes well. Choose medium to lightweight fabrics. If you use fabric that is stiff, the swag won't drape properly. Good choices include polyester satin, brushed cotton, soft denim, sheers, polyester cotton, lace, to name a few.

For a rich formal setting, you might see printed brocade draped over a pole to form swags and cascades. Another choice would be a swag and tail combination using damask fabric. Consider five swags across a series of French doors. At one time, swags and cascades graced the windows of stately mansions but these same treatments are now used in both formal and informal settings.

Two swags.

One swag.

Four swags in printed brocade.

A casual scarf swag. Scarf swags consist of one length of fabric and are a casual way to decorate a window. They are usually self-lined or lined with a contrasting fabric.

A more traditional swag. Just as the name suggests, traditional swags tend to create a traditional style for your home. These swags give the impression they are just thrown over a pole, but that is far from the truth. They are made from a square or rectangle of fabric that is pleated or gathered on the bias. It is better to use an odd number of swags so that one is centered on the window. This type of swag can be up to 48" wide. If the window is wider, use multiple swags and position them so they overlap or just touch.

Five swags across French doors.

A rod-mounted open swag.

You Will Need

* Decorator fabric (see below to calculate yardage)
* Pole and appropriate hardware
* Tape measure

Directions

1. To calculate yardage:
   a. Mount the pole on the wall.
   b. Drape a cord or tape measure across the pole. Let it drape down the amount of the depth you want the swag to be. Use the full width of the fabric.
   c. Add the desired length of the two side tails to this measurement.
   d. Wrap the fabric around the pole and allow the cascades to fall.

Tip

If you buy a commercial pattern for swags, the instructions may ask you to "level and trim the selvages on printed fabrics." This means you should lay the fabric flat and fold it in half lengthwise. Match the pattern, then draw a straight line across the width. Pin the layers together and trim along the straight line.

This simple scarf swag adds an elegant touch to the window treatment.

Photo courtesy of Graber (Hand-Carved Wood Ware by Springs Window Fashions), Middleton, Wis.

Instead of pulling and tugging the fabric to shape your swag, here's a way to pre-measure your swag so all you have to do is lay it across the swag holders. This gives you a lot less to worry about.

You Will Need

* Decorator fabric (see below to calculate yardage)
* Swag holders and appropriate hardware
* Drapery hooks
* Tape measure

Directions

1. How to calculate yardage:
   a. Secure the swag holders to the wall.
   b. Drape a cord or tape measure across the holders. Let it drape down the amount of the depth you want the swag to be. The example in the illustration uses an 18" droop. Record this measurement.
   c. Add the desired length of the two side tails to this measurement.
   d. If you want to include rosettes, add 24" for each rosette.

2. You will use the entire width of the fabric. Cut the fabric the length of the above measurement plus 1/2" for the seam allowance.

3. Measure and mark 18" from each corner of the fabric. This creates the angle necessary for the cascading pleated sides; it can change based on how much of an angle you want. Draw diagonal lines from each corner to the 18" marks. Trim away the triangular pieces.

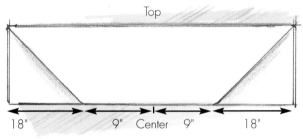

54" – the width from swag holder to swag holder.

4. Press under and stitch a narrow hem on all four sides.

5. Place the swag on the floor or work surface with the decorator fabric facing up. Find and mark the center of the panel.

6. Measure the width between the swag holders. In this example, it's 54" and we added 18" for the swag droop.

7. Mark the measurement between the swag holders on the shorter edge of the fabric piece.

8. Measure from the center mark 9" more on each side to determine where you will hand gather the fabric. Hand pinch or hand pleat from the bottom up.

9. Use masking tape to hold the gathering in position while you place the fabric swag on the swag holders.

10. Drape the swag across the swag holders.

11. Remove the tape.

Swag Ideas

* Use ornate shelf brackets for a lovely effect.
* Use brass rings – one on each end or perhaps two on the pole itself.
* Tie a knot at the end of each tail.
* Use a Shepherd's Crook decorative pole.
* Use two different fabrics for the swag and place them through the same sconces or scarf holders.
* Combine swags with tabbed draperies.
* Combine swags with sheers.
* Consider a floor-puddled swag/jabot. Simply make a swag and allow for extra fabric length in the tails for puddling. Hang the swag as usual but at sill length, gather, and tie the fabric. Allow the extra fabric to puddle on the floor.

Inspirational Potpourri

Triple swags and tails accented by jumbo cord rosettes.

Swags and teardrop-shaped tails/jabots attached to posts. For this look, swags are attached to small covered boards that are installed directly to the wall. This creates a free-floating effect.

Place fringe or cording on the swag's edge.

Photo courtesy of Graber (Hand-Carved Wood Ware by Springs Window Fashions), Middleton, Wis.

This carved wood ware pole and sconce enhance the elegant fabric of the swag.

Instead of letting the tails hang freely, use a cord to create a "bishop sleeve."

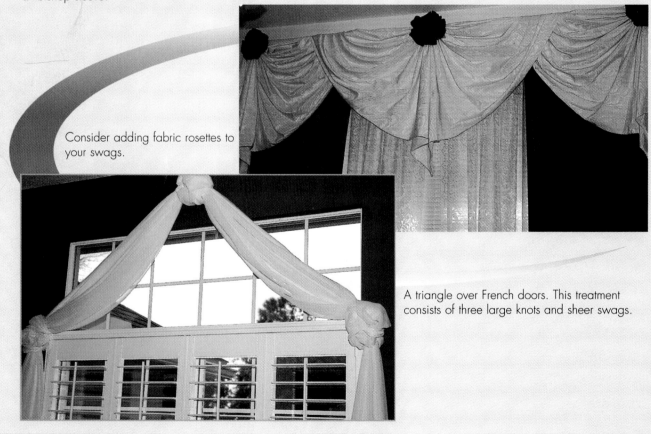

Consider adding fabric rosettes to your swags.

A triangle over French doors. This treatment consists of three large knots and sheer swags.

Formal velvet swags with ball fringe.

A single swag with contrast lined tails/jabots.

A simple swag with a fabric knot in the middle.

Three ball-shaped finials mounted in a triangle over the bed. This photo shows two swags sewn together to make one very long swag.

This simple window treatment consists of a long rectangle of fabric puddled on the floor and hung on three ball-shaped finials.

This stunning effect is simple. Just mount three sconces in a triangle configuration and thread the swag through. Combine the swag with tieback draperies.

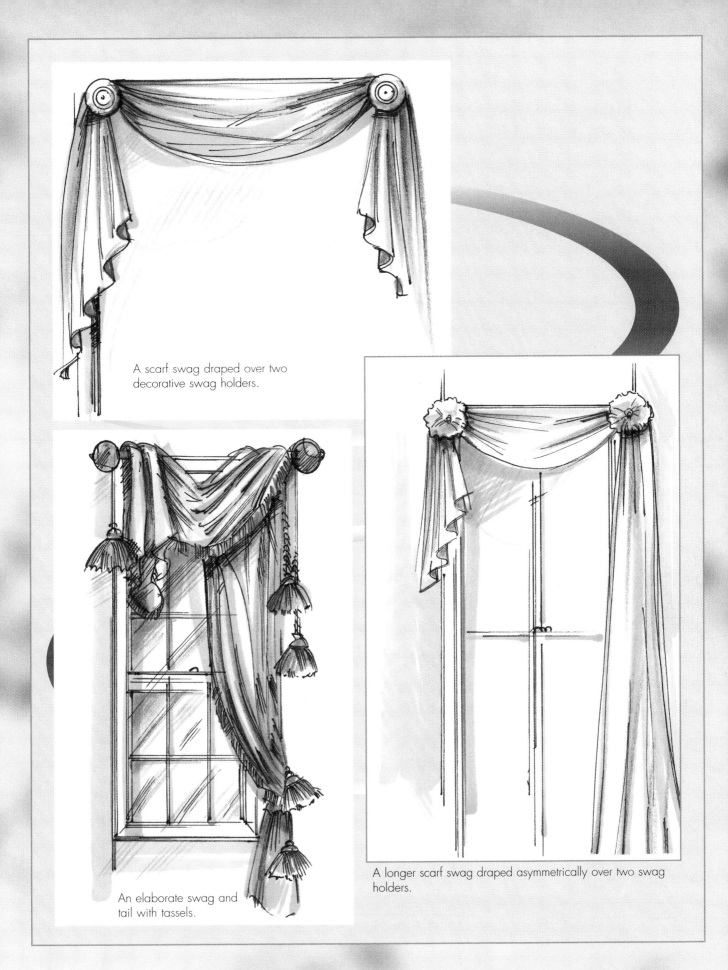

A scarf swag draped over two decorative swag holders.

An elaborate swag and tail with tassels.

A longer scarf swag draped asymmetrically over two swag holders.

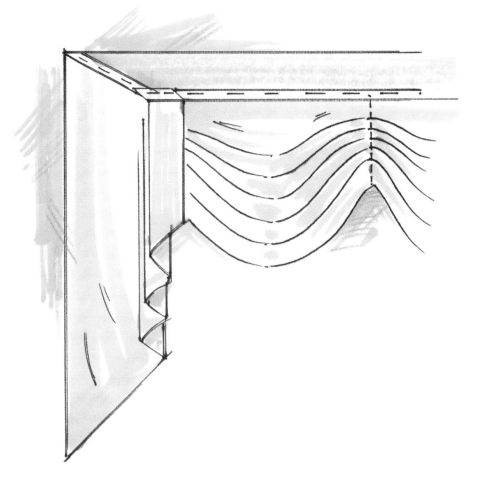

You Will Need

* Decorator fabric (see below to calculate yardage)
* Lining fabric (same amount)
* Finished swag mounted on installed mounting board

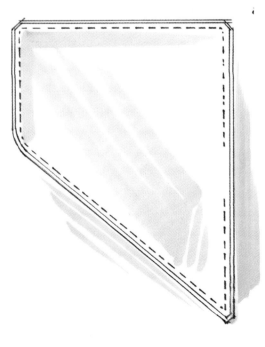

Directions

1. To calculate yardage:
  a. Use the full width of the fabric.
  b. Measure the length of the window and divide by 3. This is the finished length of the tail/jabot.
  c. The short side of the tail/jabot is 1/5 the length of the window.
  d. Add 3" to the top and bottom for the hem allowance.

2. With right sides together, stitch the decorator fabric to the lining fabric, leaving an opening for turning. Clip the corners and turn right side out. Press and slipstitch the opening closed.

3. Mark the position of the pleats on the top edge of the tail/jabot with basting stitches.

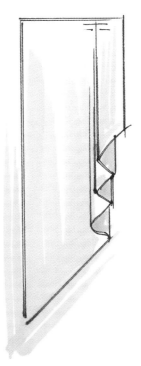

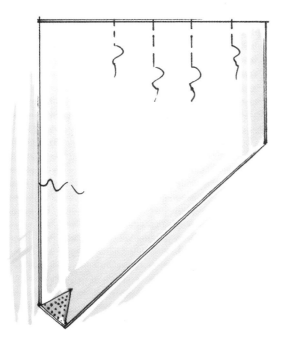

4. Start at the inner short edge and fold the pleats. You will end up with some pleats and an area that is not pleated. Hand baste or pin the pleats in place, if desired.

5. Staple a pleated tail/jabot in place on either side of the formal swag mounted on the board. The long edge of the tail/jabot should be flush with the back of the mounting board and the pleats should hang along the front of the board. Staple the upper edge of the tail/jabot 1" over the upper edge of the mounting board.

Rather than using a plain wood pole or just painting or staining the pole, try covering it with fabric. Use the same fabric to cover ball finials. This is a wonderful designer touch, and the best part is *you* are the designer.

You Will Need

* Fabric (see below to calculate yardage)
* Wood pole
* Wood ball finials
* Fabric glue or staple gun
* Rubber bands
* Decorative cord or trim

Directions

1. To cover the pole, you'll need a strip of fabric the length of the pole x the circumference of the pole plus 2". The leftover fabric will be enough to cover the ball finials.

2. Mark a line on the pole along the entire length. Place one raw edge of the fabric strip along that line and staple or glue the fabric in place.

3. Wrap the fabric around the pole. Fold under the raw edge and staple or glue the fabric in place. Apply glue around the ends of the pole so the fabric will stay in place. Let dry.

4. To cover the ball portion of the finial, measure the ball from the top to the neck and add 1". Cut one fabric circle this diameter for each finial.

5. Place the ball in the center of the fabric circle. Wrap the fabric around the ball and secure it with a rubber band. Be sure to adjust the fullness.

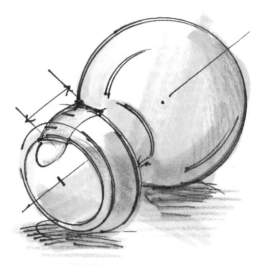

6. To cover the rest of the finial, measure from the neck to the base and add 1". Cut one fabric circle this diameter for each finial.

7. Find the center of the circle and pierce it over the screw in the end of the rod.

8. Attach the finial to the wood pole.

9. Place a small amount of glue around the finial neck and wrap the fabric circle around the neck. Secure this with a rubber band. Adjust the fullness and let the glue dry.

10. Cover the rubber band with a cord or trim.

How to Use a Swag and Tails Over Drapery Side Panels

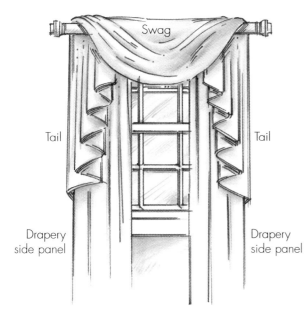

Swag

Tail

Tail

Drapery side panel

Drapery side panel

You Will Need

* Pole/rod and appropriate hardware
* Standard curtain rod and appropriate hardware
* Fabric drapery side panels
* Fabric swag and tails

Directions

1. Mount a standard curtain rod along the top of the window. This rod will be behind the pole rod. Hang the side drapery panels on the standard curtain rod.

2. Mount the pole/rod above the window. Place the swag on the pole/rod with the shorter edge down. Lap the center over the front of the rod and drape the ends of the swag over the back.

3. To create the draping at the center, pull the top (or long edge) of the swag tight along the back of the pole/rod. Holding the top edge of the swag in place at the center with one hand, use the other hand to gently pull the bottom folds down in the center to the depth desired.

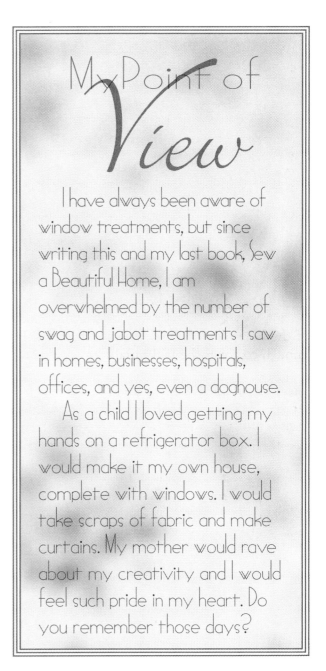

My Point of View

I have always been aware of window treatments, but since writing this and my last book, Sew a Beautiful Home, I am overwhelmed by the number of swag and jabot treatments I saw in homes, businesses, hospitals, offices, and yes, even a doghouse.

As a child I loved getting my hands on a refrigerator box. I would make it my own house, complete with windows. I would take scraps of fabric and make curtains. My mother would rave about my creativity and I would feel such pride in my heart. Do you remember those days?

Arrange the remaining folds along the center of the swag, keeping the top edge taut.

4. You can either arrange the tail ends in pleats or open them out gently for a softer look. Remember, you are the decorator. The choice is yours.

View 10

Pleated Curtains

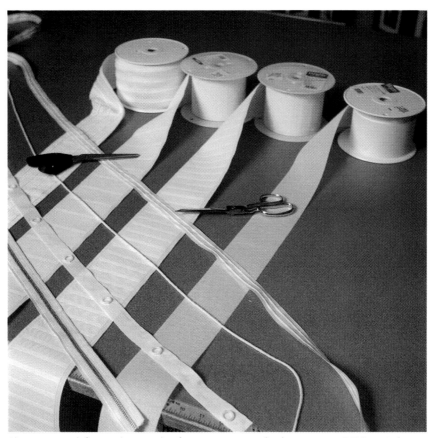

Pleater tapes left to right: spools of transparent pinch pleater tape, 3-7/8″ regular pleater tape, 3-7/8″ multi-pleater tape, iron-on pleater tape. Diagonal from top to bottom: transparent mini-pleater tape, lead weight tape, Austrian shade tape, zipper.

When making pleated window treatments, you need to decide whether or not to use pleater tapes. Using pleater tape will save you a lot of time. Pleater tapes have small pockets that create perfect sized pleats and make curtain-making almost foolproof. So why would someone start from scratch? Why do some quilters stitch their quilts by hand and some stitch them on the sewing machine? It is a matter of preference. Professional decorators rarely or never use pleater tapes because they are trained and skilled at making their own pleats.

Pleater tapes come in various widths and styles and can be used with either lined or unlined curtains. The tape is applied flat to the top of a curtain panel and when the cords are pulled, it creates the heading of the curtain. There are a multitude of pleater tapes available to create a variety of headings.

The amount of pleater tape you need is equal to the cut width of both drapes (or one long drape) plus four extra spaces. It is best to leave an unpleated space on both ends. If your drapery has a two-way draw, buy eight extra spaces.

Types of Pleater Tape

* Use narrower pleater tape for a simple gathered heading. This narrow tape helps form gathers on small-scale curtains. Allow 2-1/2 to 3 times the track length for fullness.
* For sheer or net fabrics, use sheer or net pleater tape. This type of tape will form very thin pencil pleats. You can use standard hooks or slip a curtain rod through the loops in the tape. Allow 2 to 3 times the track width for fullness (3 is better).
* Use smocking pleater tape for neatly smocked folds at the heading. This type of tape creates a lovely effect for valances and curtains. Allow 2-1/2 times the track length for fullness.
* Use 2-cord or 4-cord shirring tape for a very softly gathered heading. Allow 2-1/2 to 3 times the track length for fullness.
* Use 2-cord pencil-pleater tape to produce multiple folds. Allow 2-1/2 times the track length for fullness.
* Use triple pinch-pleater tape for full-length curtains. Allow 2 times the track length for fullness.
* Use cartridge pleater tape for cylindrical pleats. This is another tape that works well on full-length curtains. Allow 2 times the track length for fullness.
* Use box-pleater tape for curtains and valances that are never opened or closed. Allow 3 times the track length for fullness.

Applying pleater tape doesn't have to be a chore. After the curtain bottom and sides are hemmed, measure up from the bottom to the desired length and fold down the fabric on that mark. Press in place. Cut the pleater tape the width of the curtain plus 1-1/2". Place the tape below the top fold and turn the ends of the tape under 3/4", lining up the side edges. Machine stitch along the ends of the tape and across the top and bottom edges of the tape. Sew in the same direction to eliminate puckers.

Another method is to place the pleater tape at the top edge (after you have hemmed the side edges) with right sides together. Stitch across the top and turn the pleater tape to the wrong side of the curtain. Then stitch across the top and bottom of the tape and across the ends.

To gather the tape, grab the ends of the drawstrings at the side of the curtain and pull the strings in unison. This will cause the tape to gather and form pleats. Move the pleats along the length of the tape until you have the desired width. Tie the ends of the drawstrings in a slipknot. If you don't have an extra set of hands (or a very smart dog or cat), tie the strings to the leg of a table. *Caution:* Make sure the strings are securely tied off at one end before you start pulling. If they aren't, you will be very upset with yourself.

How to Make an Unlined Pleated Curtain With Pleater Tape

You Will Need

* Pole and appropriate hardware
* Decorative fabric (see below to calculate yardage)
* Pleater tape (see Step 4)
* Drapery hooks

Let's take a quick look at how to measure for this type of curtain. First consider where you want the top of the curtain to be and measure down to the desired length of the finished curtain. Most curtains look best with a double 3" bottom hem and a double 4" header at the top. In this example, the finished length is 40" and there's a double 3" bottom hem, a 4" header, and 1" double side hems. Your measurements will be different to fit your window.

Directions

1. To determine the cut length:

	Example
Start with the finished length	40"
Add double the 3" hem	+ 6"
Add double the 4" header	+ 8"
	54"

Cut the fabric 54" long.

2. The pleater tape is what determines the fullness of the curtain. Each tape is designed to give a specific fullness when the cords are drawn (see page 115). To determine the cut width of the fabric for the panel, multiply the finished window width (including the rod returns and/or overlaps) by the fullness of the tape, then add 4" for a double 1" hem on either side of the panel.

	Example
Start with the finished width	36"
Multiply by pleater tape fullness	36" x 2-1/2 = 90"
Add 2 double 1" side hems	<u>+ 4"</u>
	94"

Cut each panel 94" wide.

For center draw curtains, the same procedure would apply, but a total of 8" would be added for the side hems (double the 1" hem on each side of both panels).

3. To determine the total yardage required: Sometimes the cutting width of your drapery will exceed the width of your fabric and you will need to seam panels together to achieve the final width.
a. To determine how many panels you need, divide the drapery width by the fabric width and round up.
b. To determine how much fabric you need, multiply the number of panels by the cutting length of the drapery.
c. If your fabric has a pattern repeat, add the length of the repeat for each panel to match the design at the panel seams. For large prints, you will need to add as much as 3/4 yard for each panel.

4. The fabric width measurement is the measurement you use to determine how much pleater tape you need. Always buy a little extra so you can lay out your pleats symmetrically. (A pleat always begins and ends at the edge of each panel.) Unless absolutely unavoidable, you do not want half a pleat at the opening edge of your curtain.

5. Cut and piece the fabric to size. Remember to trim off the fabric selvages.

6. Fold and press a 1" side hem to the wrong side, then fold and press another 1" on the length of each side of the panel to form a 1" double side hem. Stitch in place.

7. Fold and press a 4" header to the wrong side, then fold and press another 4" on top of the curtain to form a 4" double header and pin in place (don't stitch yet).

8. Position the pleater tape on the header with the pastel marking line face up and at the top. Fold under the raw edge of the tape on the starting end and secure the draw cords with knots to prevent the cords from being pulled out when you are forming the pleats.

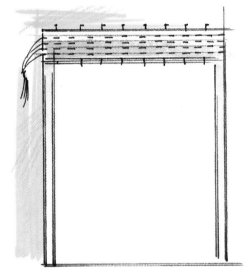

Pleater tape pinned on the wrong side of the fabric.

9. Pin the end of the tape even with the side hem on the wrong side of the curtain and down from the top of the header the desired distance.

10. On the opposite side edge, fold under 1" of the pleater tape and stitch it down to prevent fraying, being careful not to catch the draw cords in your stitching.

11. Pin the pleater tape in place along the length of the header to keep it from shifting when you sew.

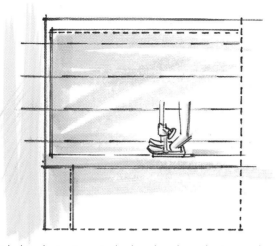

Stitch the pleater tape to the header along the top and bottom of the tape.

12. Stitch the pleater tape to the header along the top of the tape, being careful not to catch the draw cords in your stitching. Stitch again along the bottom edge of the tape, always stitching in the same direction (this is very important). You may want to add additional stitching lines in the body of the tape, depending on the design of the tape, the weight of the fabric, and the look you are trying to achieve.

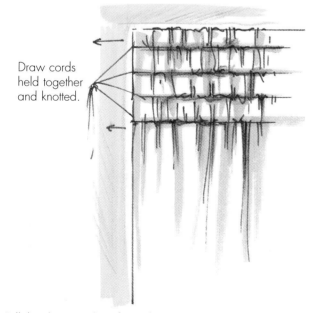

Draw cords held together and knotted.

Pull the draw cords to form pleats.

13. To achieve the best results when drawing the cords, ask someone for assistance (or train your pet). Hold the cords in one hand while moving the fabric along the cords. Don't force the pleats. The pleater tape forms the pleat. When the cords that sit on the surface of the tape disappear into the pleat without puckering, you have successfully created the perfect pleat. Knot the cords securely, close to the last pleat, and either cut off the excess cord or wrap it so you can release the knots later when laundering the curtains. I highly recommend you don't cut off the excess.

14. Insert drapery hooks into the tape and hang your curtains.

15. Always pin the hem of your curtains after they are hung to ensure that the hem will be even and the length will be perfect. You have allowed for a double 3" hem so you have room for error. After a few days have passed, take the curtains down, stitch in the hem, and re-hang.

Inspirational Potpourri

This look was created using the basic panel with an attached valance with decorative fringe. Use rings attached to the back of the panel and place the treatment on a beautiful decorative rod. This is not pleated but loosely droops for a more informal effect.

This is similar to the droop top curtain, but with no attached valance. I used lovely cut velvet to create an elegant but less structured look than traditional pleated draperies hung on rings.

How to Make a Lined Pleated Curtain With Pleater Tape

This lined drapery was made using pleater tape. The combination of the coordinating cornice and matching pillows makes a very dramatic statement.

You Will Need

* Pole and appropriate hardware
* Decorative fabric (to calculate yardage, refer to Steps 1-3 on pages 113-114)
* Lining fabric (same amount)
* Pleater tape (see Step 4 on page 114)
* Drapery hooks

1. Follow the directions for the unlined drape (page 113) but do not stitch the side hems.

2. Cut the panels for the lining 5" shorter than the curtain. Allow 3-1/2" at the hem edge and 1-1/2" at the heading. Join the panels of lining fabric with plain flat seams and trim 1-1/2" from each side of the lining panels.

3. Turn under the sides and hem of the lining by 5/8".

4. Turn the sides of the drapery fabric under and the hem up along the bottom. Stitch in place.

5. Place the lining, wrong sides together. At the sides and hem, pin, tack, and slipstitch the lining to the drapery fabric.

6. Attach the heading.

7. Continue from Step 4 of the unlined drapery (page 114) to attach the heading.

How to Add Interlining to a Curtain

Interlining a curtain provides insulation and adds durability to your drape. When adding an interlining to a lined curtain, fold and press (but don't stitch) the bottom and side hems of the drapery fabric. Open these hems out and lay the interlining on the fabric, making sure it is trimmed to fit within the hem folds. Stitch the interlining to the drapery fabric with parallel vertical rows. Proceed as you would for a lined drape.

How to Make a Lined Pleated Curtain Without Pleater Tape

You Will Need

* Rod and appropriate hardware
* Decorator fabric (see below to calculate yardage)
* Lining fabric (same amount)
* Buckram
* Drapery weights
* Wooden rings

The example shown uses a finished treatment that is 48" wide x 87" long. The rod extends 6" out on each side of the window, using a 1" traverse rod with a 2-1/2" return. It hangs 6" above the window and to the floor, creating a finished length of 87". Your measurements will be different to fit your window.

Directions

1. To determine the cut length:

	Example
Start with the finished length	87"
Add double the hem (2 x 4")	+ 8"
Add double the header (2 x 1")	+ 2"
	97"

Cut the fabric 97" long.

2. To determine the cut width:

	Example
Start with the rod measurement	48"
Multiply by 3 times fullness	x 3
	144"
Add 2 returns (2 x 2-1/2")	+ 5"
Add overlap	+ 4"
Add side hems	+ 6"
	159"

Divide by fabric width & round up   ÷ 54
(most decorator fabrics are 54" wide) 2.9444"

You will need 3 widths of fabric. Purchase extra fabric to accommodate repeats if necessary.

3. Cutting the fabric: Cut each of the 3 widths 97" long. Be sure to match your print at the seams. To avoid seams at the center, split cut one between the selvages and sew these to the outside of cuts 2 and 3. Repeat with the lining fabric except cut it 3" smaller.

4. Sewing the panels: Press up 4" at the hem and press up again. This will create a double 4" hem. Do the same for the lining using a double 3" hem.

5. Place the right side of the face fabric to the right side of the lining. The lining hem will line up 3" above the face fabric.

6. Place a piece of 4" drapery buckram on the lining side and sew all three pieces together using a 1/2" seam allowance. Turn right side out. Turn so the seam faces the fabric, which brings 1/2" of drapery fabric to the back.

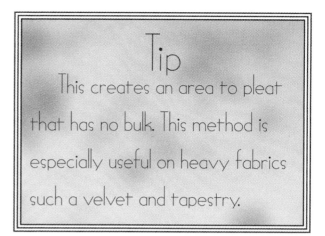

7. Press in double 1-1/2" side hems and blind or hand stitch. Insert drapery weights at the bottom corners and stitch closed.

8. To calculate the pleats for a pair of draperies:

	Example
Start with the rod measurement	48"
Add 2 returns (2 x 2-1/2")	+ 5"
Add the overlap allowance	+ 4"
	57"
Divide by 2	÷ 2
	28-1/2"

This gives you the finished width of each half of the pair needs to be.

9. A good space size between each pleat is 4". Divide the finished width by 4 to find how many spaces you need (28-1/2" ÷ 4" = 7.125) and round up. Divide 28-1/2" by 8 spaces = 3.56 or 3-5/8". When your calculations result in half a space or even a portion of a space, it means your space size will have to change. It is up to you if you choose to stay with the lesser number of spaces thus making them bigger, or add another space thus making them smaller. When another space is added, it also requires an extra pleat, so make this decision with thought as to how much fullness you have to spare. Once you decide on how many spaces you want, divide that number into the finished width size to find exactly what size your spaces need to be. Your return and overlaps will stay the same. Some of the spaces can be a bit bigger or smaller than others, if necessary.

10. Determine how many pleats are needed for that panel. When returns and overlaps are used you will always have one less pleat than you have spaces. So, in this case, if you have 8 spaces, you will have 7 pleats.

11. To find how full the pleats need to be, you need to know how much excess fabric will be in the drapery panel. Measure across the top of the drapery panel to get your flat width measurement. Take this measurement after the side hems are in and it is ready for pleating.

Subtract the finished width measurement (28-1/2") from the flat width measurement to find how much excess fabric you have for the pleats (78" – 28-1/2" = 49-1/2" fullness for pleats). 78" is the result of 54" wide fabric + half of 54" – 3" for side hems.

12. Divide the number of pleats (7) into the fullness amount to find how much fabric to put in each pleat (49-1/2" ÷ 7 = 7-1/8"). Each pleat will have 7-1/8" of fabric in it.

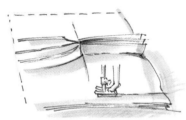

13. After determining your pleats and marking your panels as such, you are ready to sew your pleats.

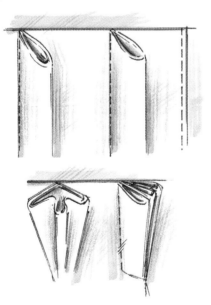

Fold the fabric as shown in the illustrations and stitch to the bottom of the pleats, using the buckram as your guide and backstitching at the top and bottom.

14. After deciding what pleat style you want (pinch, goblet, cartridge, etc.), fold your pleat and stitch the bottom of the pleat in place with a straight stitch or a wide zigzag with the stitch length set to almost zero.

15. Sew in all the pleats and measure the panels to make sure they are the correct finished size for your rod including the return and overlaps. Make any necessary adjustment by restitching one or two pleats as necessary. Some of your spaces may be slightly different but this should not be visible.

16. Stitch a wooden ring at the top of each pleat and slip the drape onto the rod.

17. Stand back and be very proud of yourself.

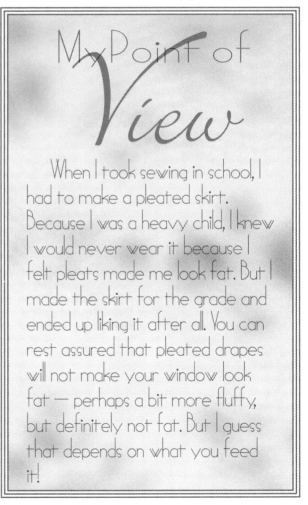

My Point of *View*

When I took sewing in school, I had to make a pleated skirt. Because I was a heavy child, I knew I would never wear it because I felt pleats made me look fat. But I made the skirt for the grade and ended up liking it after all. You can rest assured that pleated drapes will not make your window look fat — perhaps a bit more fluffy, but definitely not fat. But I guess that depends on what you feed it!

View 11

Quick & Easy Window Treatments

As a long time sewer, it's hard for me to admit that there is such a thing as "no-sew" curtains but I realize not everyone likes to sew as much as I do. Listed below are a few no-sew ideas for jazzing up your window and letting your personality shine through.

* Thread a pole through the arms of a sports jersey. Stuff the shirt, tie at the waist with a cord, and you have a great window treatment for any sports enthusiast.

* Another idea for a sports fan: hang team pennants from a wooden rod.
* Use painted clothespins to hang a shawl on a cord across the window.
* For a bright and colorful look, hang plastic strips from a wooden rod the width of the window.
* If you have a beach house, try beach mats hung from a rod. They can be easily rolled up and tied.

How to Make a Two-Rod Shirred Curtain

In the example shown, the rods are 30" wide and the finished sheer is 72" long. The side hems are 3" and the top and bottom headers are 1". These measurements are for illustrative purposes. Your measurements will be different to fit your window.

You Will Need

* 2 standard curtain rods and appropriate hardware
* Fabric (see below to calculate yardage)

Directions

1. To determine how many fabric widths you need:

	Example
Start with the width of the rod	30"
Multiply this amount by 3 for fullness	x 3
	90"
Add 2 side hems (2 x 3")	+ 6"
	96"
Divide by fabric width & round up (fabric shown is 118" wide)	÷ 118
	0.813

You will need 1 width of fabric.

Beautiful, soft sheers cover the powder room door. You often see sheers on doors to allow light to come through while providing privacy.

2. To determine the cut length:

	Example
Start with the finished length	72"

Add double the top & bottom rod
  pockets   + 6"
(3/4" rods require 1-1/2" pockets, so 2 x 3")

Add double the top & bottom headers
  (2 x 2")   <u>+ 4"</u>
                                         82"

Cut the fabric 82" long.

3. To determine the total yardage required:

	Example
Start with the number of widths (from Step 1)	1
Multiply times the cut length (from Step 2)	x 82"
Divide by 36 & round up	<u>÷ 36</u>
	2.28"

You will need 2-1/2 yards of fabric.

4. Sewing the curtain: Fold the side edges of the fabric in 1-1/2" and press. Fold over again and stitch in the side hems.

5. Turn the top and bottom edges under 2-1/2" and press. Fold under another 2-1/2" on each end and stitch in your rod pocket across the full width of the fabric close to the crease to form the top and bottom hems.

6. On the top and bottom, measure down 1" from the fold of the fabric and sew across the full width on both ends. This creates a 1" header and 1-1/2" pocket for the top and bottom rods.

7. Slide the top and bottom rods into their pockets. Hang the top rod first.

8. Stretch the curtain down until the material is tight. Mark the location on the wall where the bottom rod should be installed. Install the bottom brackets at this point. Pull the curtain tight and slide the bottom rod onto the brackets. You now have a two-rod shirred curtain.

Hang pennants over a full-length curtain or on a valance to give you a casual, fun look. The fabric pennants can be made of contrasting fabrics, a print, or even a plaid. Remember, you are the designer.

You Will Need

* Decorator fabric (determined by the size of the pennants you are making)
* Lining fabric (same amount)
* Craft paper
* Optional: tassels

Directions

1. Decide how many pennants you want. Using brown craft paper and a straight edge, determine the size of the pennants you desire and make a paper pattern. Be sure to include 1/2" seam allowances.

2. Using your paper pattern, cut the desired number of pennants from the decorator fabric. Do the same with the lining.

3. Cut two tabs for each pennant from the decorator fabric only.

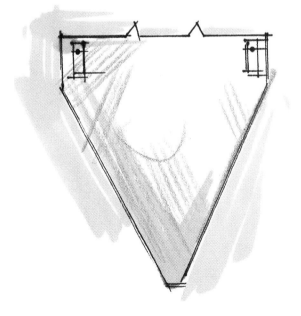

4. Fold the tab in half lengthwise and stitch on the long edge. Turn and press.

5. Fold the tab piece in half and pin it on the right side of each outer edge of the decorator pieces as shown.

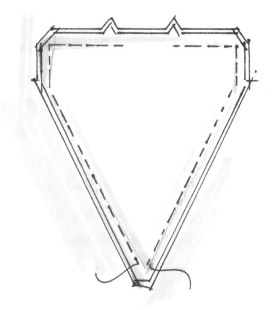

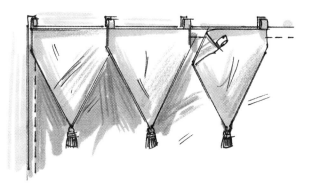

8. Place the pennants next to each other, butting them up together, along the width of the curtain panel.

9. Thread the pole through the tabs. When the curtain panel is pushed to the side, you will get a teardrop effect.

6. With right sides together, sew the lining and fabric pieces together, leaving an opening for turning. If you want to add a tassel, do so on the point before stitching.

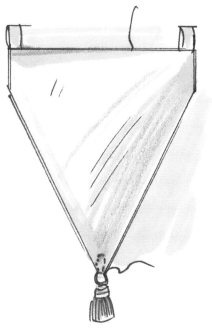

7. Trim the seams, clip the corners, and turn right side out. Press, then slipstitch the opening closed.

Inspirational Potpourri

Instead of making tabs and hanging the pennants on a pole, here they are hung with the curtain panel. A child's point of view.

Pennants of coordinating fabric in varying lengths hung over a fabric valance.

Another formation of pennants over a fabric valance.

How to Make a Tent Flap Window Treatment

A tent flap valance in a bright and sunny room.

In the tent flap treatment shown, the fabric extends 2" out on each side of the window. A 1" x 2" board was hung 2" above the window and the fabric hangs to the bottom of the 48" window. These measurements are for illustrative purposes only. Your measurements will be different to fit your window.

You Will Need

* Decorator fabric #1 (see below to calculate yardage)
* Decorator fabric #2 (see below to calculate yardage)
* 1" x 2" mounting board the width of the finished treatment
* Appropriate hardware to mount the board to the window or wall
* Rings (2 for each window)
* Cup hooks (2 for each window)
* Tassel on cord
* Staple gun or glue

Directions

1. To determine **how wide** to cut the fabric:

	Example
Measure the exact width of the mounting board	40"
Divide in half	÷ 2
	20"
Add 1/2" seam allowance on each side	+ 1"
	21"

Cut the fabric 21" wide.

2. To determine **how long** to cut the fabric:

	Example
Start with the finished length	50"
Add 1-1/2" to put on the board	+ 1-1/2"
Add 1/2" for seam allowance	+ 1/2"
	52"

Cut the fabric 52" long.

3. Cutting the fabric: You will make two fabric sections for each window. Cut two pieces of fabric #1 and two of fabric #2 for each window.

4. Sewing the fabric pieces: With the right sides of fabric #1 and fabric #2 together, sew the two sides and the bottom of each piece, leaving the top open.

5. Clip the corners, turn the piece right side out, and press. Serge or zigzag the top closed.

6. Cover the board with a scrap of one of the fabrics just in case a little of it peeks out at the center. Alternatively, you could paint the board to coordinate with the fabric.

7. Staple the tent fabric pieces to the board on the 1" edge (think of it as a shelf).

8. Hold the board in position on your window to determine how much window you want exposed. This will determine the placement of a ring to pull the tent flap open. Sew the ring on the fabric piece.

9. Mount the board to the window or wall.

10. Put a cup hook on the wall to hold the ring.

11. Secure a tassel to the ring for a great decorator touch.

When pulled together, the flaps show the contrasting lining fabric.

This treatment was made using a sheer unlined panel attached to a board. A beautiful fringe was attached along one side and the bottom. Decorative cord of varying lengths was attached to the board, evenly spaced across the top. Then the other end of the cord was attached to the sides of the panel at even increments.

This look can be achieved by using purchased panels or making a simple unlined panel. The amount of cord is determined by the width of the window and how many pull-ups you want.

Photo courtesy of Graber (Hand-Carved Wood Ware by Springs Window Fashions), Middleton, Wis.

What a simple way to achieve this fabulous effect! Hang a basic panel with rings and sew one ring to the corner to pull up.

Decorative tassels at each pull-up point.

You Will Need

* Fabric (45" wide)
  2-1/2 yards for 36" finished length
  3 yards for 45" finished length
  3-1/2 yards for 54" finished length
  4 yards for 63" finished length
* 1/2 yard additional matching or contrasting
  fabric for tabs

Directions

1. For 36" finished length, cut 2 panels each 42" in length.
For 45" finished length cut 2 panels each 51" in length.
For 54" finished length cut 2 panels each 60" in length.
For 63" finished length cut 2 panels each 69" in length.

2. Cut 12 tabs, 4" wide x 7" long.

3. Double hem each side edge, turning under 2" for a 1" finished hem.

4. Finish the upper edge of the panel by turning the edge down 1/2" and 1/2" again and stitch.

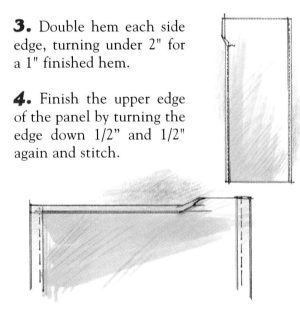

5. With right sides together fold the tab in half. Stitch the edges together. Turn right side out and press.

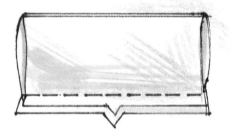

6. Fold the tab in half again, bringing the raw ends together. Baste these edges together.

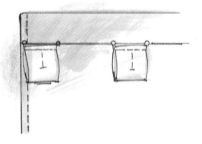

7. On the outside of the panel, arrange half the tabs along the fold with right sides together. Place the cut edge of the tabs along the fold line, with the tabs below the line. Pin in place.

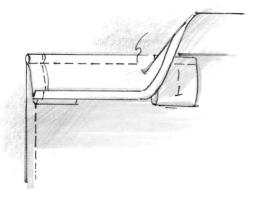

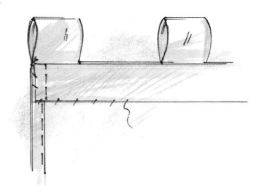

8. To create the facing, with right sides together, fold the upper edge of the panel along the fold line, encasing the raw ends of the tabs. Stitch along the upper edge 1/2" from the folded edge, being sure to catch in tabs.

9. Press the facing to the wrong side, pressing the tabs up. Hand or machine stitch the facing in place close to the inner and side edges.

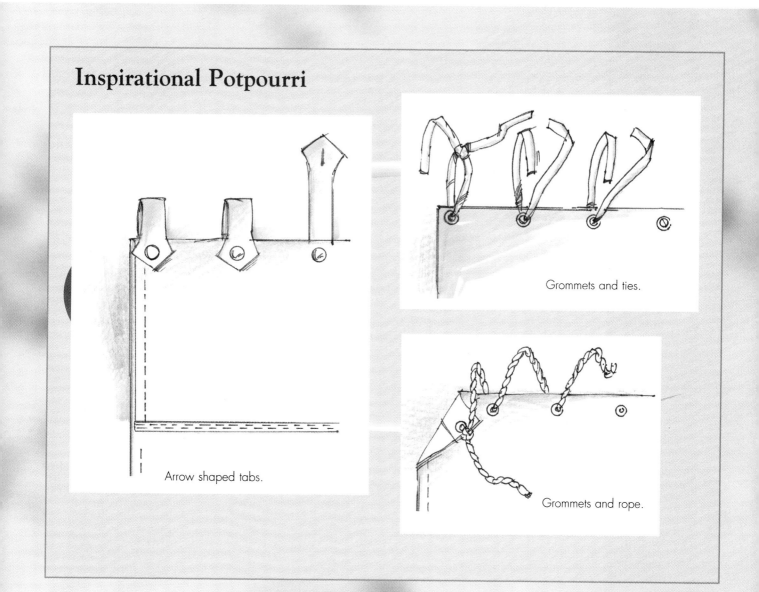

Inspirational Potpourri

Arrow shaped tabs.

Grommets and ties.

Grommets and rope.

Using the basic instructions for tab-top panels, you can make large oversized tabs that finish at 8" wide. Then make a tube from an 8" x 10" piece of fabric. After turning the tube, on the completed tab-top panel, thread each tab through the fabric tube and scrunch the tube down to create the cummerbund effect. Another idea would be to use coordinating tassels or chair ties to pull the tabs together to create the cummerbund effect.

A tabbed drapery hung on a leaf pole. To allow in more light, the drape is held back by antique brass holdbacks.

Again, the basic tab curtain using long ties to create bows at the top of the rod. Contrast fabric was used here for the banding, tieback, and tab ties, but a beautiful ribbon or cord could also be used.

This effect was achieved by using the basic instructions for tab-top panels and piecing together three different fabrics with a contrast welt between each seam. Then the panel was constructed as usual and three triangles were made using the same contrast welt. Contrasting ties attached to the top of the panel complete the look.

Another slouched drapery hung with rings instead of tabs. The matching fringe and the decorative rod make a striking statement.

Instead of using tabs to hang this crinkled silk drape, we used rings. This creates a decorative slouch effect and the bullion fringe completes the opulent look.

My Point of View

Remember the scene in the "Sound of Music" where Julie Andrews used the curtains to make the Von Trapp children new clothes? People who lived through the Depression could probably share a similar story. We need to appreciate fabric.

View 12

Shades, Blinds
& Verticals

would be irresponsible if I didn't include a chapter on shades, blinds, and verticals. Window treatments do not always stand alone – along with your new fabric window treatment, you often need a way to keep the room dark or create a feeling of total privacy. Shades and blinds are great ways to do this. If using blinds, you can choose from metal, vinyl, fabric-covered, or wood in horizontal, vertical, and mini, to name just a few variations. When you go shopping for blinds, be sure to take a swatch of your window treatment fabric with you. The choices of woods and colors are endless and there is a style to go with every personality and decorating scheme.

Shades

At times shades are your best solution for odd-shaped windows.

Everyone remembers traditional roller shades – those generic white plastic or paper window coverings that did the job but didn't add much style to the window or room. Well, roller shades have "come a long way baby." They can now be found in European florals, chic linen textures, cottage prints, and a multitude of colors ranging from tranquil shades to bright tones. Instead of a straight edge at the bottom, they now come in a variety of decorative edges. And to top all this off, shade pulls have become like pieces of jewelry. Roller shade fabrics are no longer plastic, but 100% polyester. Because of that, they can look like linen fabrics, plisse fabrics, latticework, tweeds, country prints, and even embroidered eyelet. Plastic is out, fabric is in.

To measure your window for a shade, use a steel measuring tape. For an outside mount (see page 88), measure between the points where the brackets will be mounted to the wall. Try to have the shade extend beyond the glass by at least 3" on each side. I generally recommend mounting shades on the outside of the window to get better coverage.

For an inside mount (see page 88), measure the exact opening size. The shade should be slightly narrower for an easy fit.

To calculate the length for shades, measure from the top of the shade to the hem. Shades come in prepackaged lengths. Buy one longer than you need.

A traditional roller shade with a decorative edge.

Blinds provide great privacy, light control, and can be easily opened and closed. These are often referred to as Venetian blinds, named after the early Venetian traders who brought them to Europe. In fact, it was the Persians in Italy who actually invented these blinds and at the time they were called "persiani" blinds.

Blinds are available as maxis or minis. Maxi-blinds have bigger slats, either 2" or 3" wide. Mini-blinds have slats that are 1/2" or 1" wide. You will find blinds in vinyl, wood, aluminum, fabric, and yes, even PVC. Even the string that runs through the slats (called a ladder) can be decorative. In addition to the ladder, you have a wand that controls the amount of light allowed in.

For blinds mounted outside the window (see page 88), measure the width of the opening and add at least 1-1/2" on each side for the overlap. Measure the height from the top of the frame to the sill or 1-1/2" below the opening if there is no sill. Add 1-1/2" to the height to mount the blind above the trim.

To mount blinds inside the window frame (see page 88), measure the window width at the top, center, and bottom and use the narrowest dimension. Measure the height from the inside top of the opening to the sill. If you prefer the blind not to touch the sill, deduct 1/4". Measure the height from the top of the frame to the sill or 1-1/2" below the opening if there is no sill. Add 1-1/2" to the height to mount the blinds above the trim.

You can also buy cellular blinds, also called honeycomb or pleated blinds. These are very lightweight and versatile. The pocket in these blinds traps air that insulates your windows without weight and bulk so your room will be warmer in the winter and cooler in the summer. They too come in a variety of textures and colors. Measure for these the same as you would maxi or mini blinds.

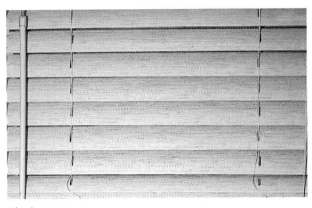

Blinds.

Blinds with a decorative ladder and cornice.

A cellular shade.

Verticals

Vertical blinds in dramatic black, topped with a coordinating swag.

Left stack verticals.

Right stack verticals.

Split draw verticals.

Center stack verticals.

Vertical blinds are a simple solution for challenging large windows. These blinds have vertical slats that can be 2" to 3-1/2" wide. They are attached to a valance and are often connected at the bottom by a plastic chain. Vertical blinds provide proportion and balance.

You'll often see this type of blind mounted at sliding doors because they can be pulled back during the day. What makes vertical blinds great is that you can keep them pulled shut but with the verticals angled to let in a little light, or pull them open halfway, or any position in-between. If the area is very large, consider motorized verticals for ease in opening and closing.

Verticals come in texture-rich knits, linens, vinyls, natural fibers, stripes, and more. Vinyl verticals are the least expensive and are available in textured, pearlized, sculpted, and a flat/curved style. The textured style can be ribbed, the pearlized style has a soft iridescent finish, and the sculpted style comes in various shapes that give you the feeling of layering. The flat style has a tendency to twist but the curved style succeeds in giving you a softer look. Verticals can be made from aluminum or covered with fabric or wallpaper.

Part of planning for verticals is knowing where you want them to stack – left, right, split draw, or center. Obviously this depends on the room.

There's such a huge variety of blinds available, I urge you to check out samples at your local dealer.

The soft shade pictured extends 2" out on each side of the window and hangs 6" above and 12" below the window, creating an 18" soft shade. Attach the soft shade to a 1" x 4" x 40" wide board with 3-1/2" returns. These measurements are for illustrative purposes. Your measurements will be different to fit your window.

You Will Need

* Decorator fabric (see below to calculate yardage)
* Lining fabric (same amount)
* 1" x 4" board x the width of finished treatment
* Appropriate hardware to mount the board

Directions

1. To determine **how wide** to cut the fabric:

	Example
Measure the board width	40"
Add 2 returns (2 x 3-1/2")	+ 7"
Add 1/2" seam allowance for each side	+ 1"
	48"

Cut the fabric 48" wide.

2. To determine **how long** to cut the fabric:

	Example
Start with the finished length	18"
Add 2" to put on the board	+ 2"
Add 12" for fullness at the bottom	+ 12"
Add 1/2" for seam allowance	+ 1/2"
	32-1/2"

Cut the fabric 32-1/2" long.

3. When cutting the fabric to size (48" wide x 32-1/2" long) be sure to center the design if your fabric has a design. Cut the lining the same size.

4. Sewing the valance: With right sides of the decorator and lining fabrics together, sew around three sides using a 1/2" seam allowance. Leave the top open.

5. Clip the corners, turn right side out, and press. Serge or zigzag the top closed.

6. Staple the fabric to the board.

7. Determine where to position the ties and staple two tassels on the board. A variety of items can be used as ties. You can make ties from contrasting fabric or use ribbons, belts, or purchased cords. Use your imagination. For this example, two large drapery tassels were taken apart to make a long cord with a tassel at each end. They were then cut apart at the center, creating four pieces.

8. Staple two additional tassels to the board over the soft shade.

9. Tie the soft shade up as shown in the photo. Hand pleat the bottom as desired.

10. Mount the board.

Inspirational Potpourri

This soft shade is pulled up with double-tassel ties to soften the look of the bathroom window.

How to Hang a Soft Shade Under a Swag and Jabots/Tails

The sheer soft shade pictured under the floral swag is 36" wide x 42" long. These measurements are for illustrative purposes. Your measurements will be different to fit your window.

You Will Need

* Fabric swag with tails mounted on window
* Sheer fabric for soft shade (see below to calculate yardage)
* 1" x 2" board x the width of the window
* Mounting board and appropriate hardware
* L-brackets for mounting the board
* Plastic rings
* Electrician's cable ties

Directions

1. To determine the **cut length**:

	Example
Start with the finished length	42"
Add 18" for fullness	+ 18"
Add 1 double bottom hem (2 x 1-1/2")	+ 3"
Add 2" for the board	+ 2"
	65"

Cut the fabric 65" long.

2. To determine the **cut width**:

	Example
Start with the finished width	36"
Add 2 double side hems (2 x 3")	+ 6"
	42"

Since this is inset in the window, there are no returns.

Cut the fabric 42" wide.

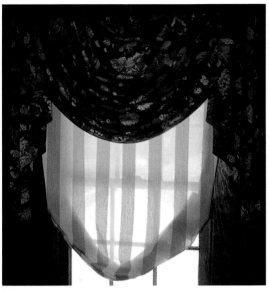

The stationary sheer soft shade under the swag and jabots filters the light in this stairwell window.

3. You need 65" of fabric or approximately 2 yards.

4. Cut fabric to size (42" wide x 65" long).

5. For the side hems, turn under 1-1/2" and press. Turn under another 1-1/2" and stitch.

6. For the bottom hem, turn under 1-1/2" and press. Turn under another 1-1/2" and stitch.

7. Staple the fabric to the 1" x 2" board.

8. Sew rings on the side hems of the shade 6" apart up the side. The number you use will determine the length. In the example pictured, there are 3 rings on each side.

9. Secure the rings together using cable ties found at a hardware store.

10. Install the treatment on L-brackets under the existing swag and jabot treatment and enjoy this fabulous look.

Stagecoach shades are a great way to add color (or colors) to a room. The dramatic dark blue shade and the red contrast lining and ties coordinate beautifully with the furniture in the room. The shade is 40" wide and 20" long mounted on a 1" x 3" x 40" board.

You Will Need

* Mounting board and appropriate hardware to mount board
* Decorator fabric (see below to calculate yardage)
* Contrasting lining and tie fabric (same amount + ties, see Step 3)
* 1" dowel or small PVC pipe the width of mounting board less 1/2"
* Double stick carpet tape
* Staple gun

Directions

1. To determine the **cut length**:

	Example
Start with the finished length	20"
Add 2" to mount on the board	+ 2"
Add 12" for the roll-up	+ 12"
Add 1/2" seam allowance	+ 1/2"
	34-1/2"

Cut the fabric 34-1/2" long.

2. To determine the **cut width**:

	Example
Start with the finished width	40"
Add 2 returns (2 x 2-1/2") (the width of the mounting board)	+ 5"
Add 2 side seam allowances (2 x 1/2") (1 for each side)	+1"
	46"

Cut the fabric 46" wide.

3. Cutting the ties. Cut four ties (more if your shade is wider), double the length of your finished valance (20" x 2 = 40") and double the desired width plus seam allowance.

4. Cut the contrasting lining the same as in Steps 1 and 2.

5. Lay the decorator fabric right side up on a flat work surface. Place the lining on top with the right side down.

6. To create the area to roll-up, you will need to make a notch on the bottom right and left side, keeping the return in place. Measure up from the bottom the amount of the roll-up (12") and mark. Do this on both sides. Now measure and mark from the sides the amount of the return and seam allowances (2 1/2 + 1/2" = 3"). Draw a line connecting these two markings. Cut out this area. This will give you an area that will roll up on your dowel or PVC pipe. When I think about this, it resembles a football goal post.

7. Sewing your seam. Leaving the top open, sew down the sides, pivot, and sew at the notched area, sewing across the bottom and up the other side.

8. Clip the corners on the bottom and notched area, and turn and press.

9. Serge or clean finish the top seam.

10. Sew the ties together. Turn and press.

11. Cover the mounting board with scrap fabric.

12. Lay the shade on a flat surface.

13. Measure and mark the spacing for the first two ties. In the example the ties are 9" from each side. Staple the ties in place on the board. Staple the shade to the top of the mounting board. Place the remaining two ties on top of the shade and staple in place. This will give you a shade sandwich – ties, valance and ties again.

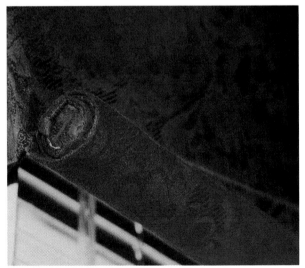

Roll up the shade to the notched edge.

14. You may want to cover the ends of the dowel or PVC with scrap fabric to keep the ends from peeking out. Attach double stick carpet tape to the dowel and carefully lay the dowel across the bottom edge of the shade. Evenly roll up the shade to the notched edge.

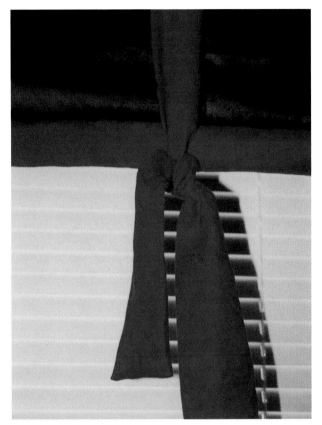

The ties hold the shade up.

15. Tie a knot in the ties to keep the dowel in place.

16. Mount the board on the wall or window frame.

Inspirational Potpourri

This variation of the stagecoach shade is hung on an oar instead of a mounting board.

This close-up shows the ropes that were used to hang the shade and the contrasting pennants.

Roman shades can be made or purchased. When you make your own you feel a great sense of accomplishment. These shades give you a visual escape from the norm and create an atmosphere filled with possibilities.

Roman shades are perfect for privacy and light control. They can be lined for extra warmth. They actually are relatively simple to make, so don't be apprehensive about making your own.

Select your fabrics carefully. Any woven furnishing fabric is a good choice. Stay away from floral patterns because it will appear too busy. A plain or geometric print works well. A fabric that holds its shape will give you crisp folds.

In this example, the mounting board is 36" wide and the finished shade is 45" long. These measurements are for illustrative purposes. Your measurements will be different to fit your window.

You Will Need

* Mounting board: 1" x 2" cut to the finished width of the shade less 1/4"
* Appropriate hardware to mount board to wall
* Fabric (see below to calculate yardage)
* Lining fabric (same amount)
* Snap tape equal to length of mounting board + 3"
* Ring tape the cutting length of the shade + 5" x the number of rows needed. To determine the number of rows needed, plan a row of tape at each edge of the shade and approximately every 10" in between. Divide the width of the window by 10, rounding up to the nearest whole number
* Polyester cord: 2 x the cutting length of the shade + the cutting width of the shade x the number of rows
* Metal rod or wooden dowel cut 1/2" shorter than the finished shade width

* L-brackets (2, depending on the width)
* T-square
* Metal screw eyes equal in number to rows of ring tape
* Cord cleat
* Staple gun or glue

Directions

1. I recommend you mount Roman shades outside rather than inside your window frame (see page 88). Measure the width of the opening and add at least 1-1/2" on each side for overlap. Measure from the top of the frame to the sill or 1-1/2" below the opening if there is no sill. If you choose an inside mount, measure the width at the top, center, and bottom and use the narrowest dimension. Shades are made slightly narrower for an easy fit. Measure the height from inside the top of the opening to the sill. A 1-3/8" deep recess is needed for a flush mounting.

2. To determine **how wide** to cut the fabric:

	Example
Start with the finished width	36"
Add 2 double 1" side hems	+ 4"
	40"

Cut the fabric 40" wide. If your fabric isn't wide enough and you have to seam panels together, divide the cut width of the Roman shade by the fabric width to get the number of panels needed (round up to the nearest whole number).

3. To determine **how long** to cut the fabric:

	Example
Start with the finished length	45"
Add 2" for the bottom hem	+ 2"
Add 2" for the board	+ 2"
	49"

Cut the fabric 49" long.

4. To determine the **total yardage** required, multiply the number of panels by the finished cutting length. *Note:* If your fabric has a pattern repeat, you need to add the length of the repeat for each panel to have enough fabric to match the design at the panel seams.

5. Cut the fabric panels to size. Cut the lining pieces the same size.

6. With right sides together, pin the fabric to the lining at the long side edges. Check and make sure you have a perfect rectangle by using a T-square, then stitch the top and side seams and press the seams open. Don't turn to the right side. *Note:* When making Roman shades, keep the stitching lines absolutely straight. Any variation from that will give you a distorted shade.

7. With right sides together, stitch the bottom seam, leaving a small opening to turn. Turn the shade to the right side and slip stitch the opening closed. Press all the edges.

8. Turn up 2" on the bottom edge and press. Do not stitch.

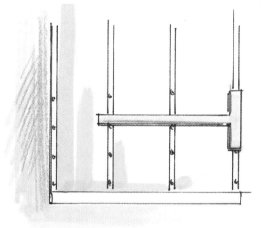

9. Pin ring tape to the lining side of the shade vertically along the side edges and evenly spaced across the width of the shade. Cut and position each tape so the bottom ring is 1" above the folded hem and the tape extends 1" into the hem. Use the T-square to make sure the tape strips are parallel.

10. Using the zipper foot, stitch the long side edges of the ring tapes through the lining and fabric. Mark the vertical position of the tapes. Run a thin line of dots of fabric glue along the lines just marked. Align the rings and press the tapes in place. Secure with pins.

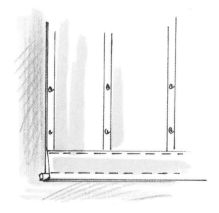

11. Stitch the hemmed bottom edge of the shade, catching the tape ends in the stitching. Slip the rod into the hem. Pin, mark, and stitch a second row of stitching, measuring evenly from the folded edge. This will hold the rod in position.

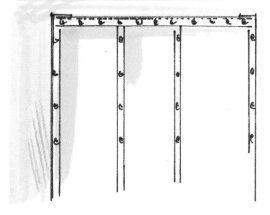

12. Separate the snap tape and pin one side to the top of the shade over the edges of the ring tape, centering the snaps on the shade and turning under 1/2" on both ends. Stitch all the edges of the snap tape through all thicknesses.

Mounting the Board and Shade

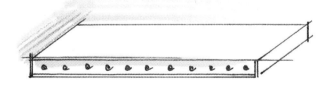

13. Consider covering the mounting board with your shade fabric. Staple the remaining side of the snap tape to the narrow edge of the mounting board. Be sure to center the snaps and turn under 1/2" on both ends.

14. Snap the shade in place.

15. Attach screw eyes to the underside of the board, directly in line with each row of ring tape.

16. In equal lengths, cut polyester cord for each row of ring tape. Tie the polyester cord to the bottom ring of the ring tape. Thread the cord up through all the rings in that row. Thread the cord through the screw eye at the top of the row and through the screw eyes to one side of the shade. Repeat for each row of ring tape.

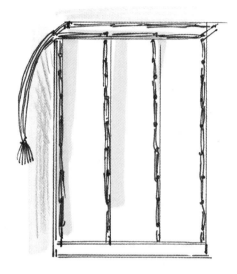

17. With the shade flat, knot the cords together just outside the last screw eye. Knot the cords again approximately 3/4 down the length of the shade.

18. Install a cleat to the window molding at a comfortable height. Twist the cords around the cleat to anchor when the shade is lifted.

Inspirational Potpourri

This mock Roman valance has a tab top.

The close-up of the mock Roman valance allows you to see the embroidered braid used as an accent.

A Roman shade looks great on a smaller window.

My Point of View

If you are moving into a new home and don't want to rush to a decision about your window treatments, put up mini-blinds to buy some time. It beats hanging a big sheet over the window.

View 13
Tiebacks & Trims

Nothing can add instant charm faster than a tieback. Let your imagination run wild and just create to your heart's content. You can use beads, buttons, antique pins, and of course, trims. I recently saw a unique tieback in a magazine that really caught my eye – an antique decorative silver spoon bent to form a perfect holdback.

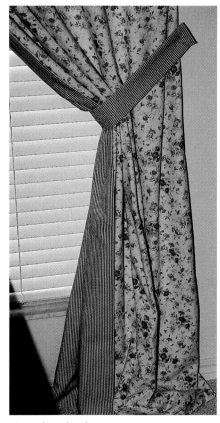

Straight tieback.

Tassel tieback.

Bow tieback.

Bullion fringe tieback.

The style of tieback you create is only limited by your imagination. Just a few possibilities include:
* Braided tiebacks
* Shirred tiebacks
* Ruffled tiebacks
* Straight tiebacks
* Pleated tiebacks
* Bow tiebacks
* Tasseled tiebacks
* Bullion fringe tiebacks
* Self-covered tiebacks
* Rope and tassel tiebacks

Adding cording or fringe to these options creates even more choices.

In a practical manner, tiebacks hold the curtain back from the window so the light can come in. In a decorative manner, they add color and contrast to your window treatment. Because a tieback lifts the curtain, it also allows the lining to show, so if you want to add a distinctive lining, tiebacks are a good way to make sure it will be noticed.

Where you position the tieback makes a difference and the proper positioning for the hooks that will support the tieback takes a little preplanning. The most common rule of thumb is to place the tieback three feet off the floor, which is usually 2/3 down from the top. Keep in mind that the hook may need to be placed higher if you are using a loose tieback. When the curtain drapes over the tieback it falls even lower. If you want the window to appear taller, place the tieback higher. If you want the window to appear wider, place the tieback lower. The window hasn't changed, but the optical illusion has.

Tiebacks are most commonly used on drapes that are going to remain stationary. The tieback needs to be correctly placed and the curtain "fluffed" so it hangs properly. This is not something you would want to do each morning when you open the curtains. (Women understand – their list of to-do's is already long in the morning.)

To determine the right length for the tieback, allow the curtain to hang for a few days, then place a tape measure around the curtain in the position you prefer. Hold the ends of the tape measure against the wall where the hook will be. Adjust the curtain over the tape measure (this is best done with a helper – another occasion for a smart dog or cat). While the helper holds the tape measure, stand back and decide whether the tape needs to be tighter or looser. Note the correct length and add 2" for the final measurement. If you are using rope or tassels, allow for twice the measurement around the curtain's fullness.

Self-covered tieback.

Rope and tassel tieback.

Yardage Requirement

Length of tieback	Amt. of fabric for a pair	If using piping
22"-24"	16"	3-1/4 yds.
30"-31"	20"	4 yds.
33"-39"	31"	4-1/4 yds.
47"-55"	36"-39"	6-1/2 yds.

Adding trim is a great way to enhance the style and character of your curtains. You can use braid, ribbon, fringe, piping, cord, binding, and tassels to give dimension to a hem or other edges. By using trim you add contrasting color and texture to your window treatment.

When adding trim to a curtain or valance, remember to match the weights of the fabric with the weight of the trim. Don't use a heavy fringe on a sheer fabric.

Trim choices are endless, so you shouldn't have any trouble finding just the right one. Trims are sold under various names – cording, braid, gimp, tassels, welting, eyelet, and fringe.

Cording/piping can be made from a variety of materials: ribbon, lace, leather, suede, or bias tape. Cording is a rope made of twisted fibers. If the cording is lipped, it has a narrow flange that allows you to sew the cord into a seam.

Cording.

Braid is flat and typically used as a border. Both edges are finished and it is usually 1" to 3" wide.

Braid.

Gimp is a looped or scalloped border that is considered a narrow braid.

Tassels.

Tassels come in a huge variety of styles – key tassels, raffia tassels, wool tassels, and swag tassels, to name just a few. This hanging ornament is made by binding strands of yarn at one end. Tassel tiebacks are very popular. They consist of tassels that are connected to a looped cord or rope and are used to hold back the curtain. There are endless colors to choose from.

Welting is fabric-covered cording that varies in width from 1/4" to 1". A narrow flange is connected so it can be sewn into a seam. Double welting is a double cord that is knitted together. Double welting is usually glued in place on upholstered projects.

Eyelet is a fabric trim that can be flat or ruffled. The most notable characteristic is the small holes that can be used to thread ribbon through.

Fringe has short strands of yarn along one edge. You can jazz up any fabric by using fringe. The texture alone adds interest. To give a valance a tailored effect, stitch the fringe to the valance so the lower edge of the fringe is level with the lower edge of the valance. There are multitudes of colors, styles, and textures to choose from when shopping for fringe.

Rope/bullion fringe.

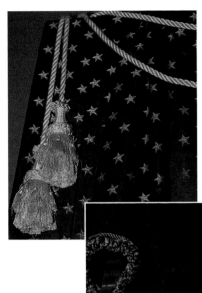
In tassel bullion fringe, the yarn strands and tassels are combined into one.

Loop fringe.

Tassel fringe.

Ball fringe.

My Point of *View*

Trims and braids can transform a humdrum curtain into a designer's dream. We live in an era where there is no end to trim choices. Go to the home decorating department at the fabric store and just stand back and gawk. There are tassels, flat braids, rope trims, bullion trims, jumbo fringes, and all in an endless array of colors and textures. Next to choosing the fabric, this will be your second biggest decision when making window treatments.

About the Author

Sally Cowan is the author of *Sew a Beautiful Home*, a television personality, sewing expert, syndicated columnist, motivational speaker, wife, stepmother, and mentor. She is an inspiring and motivating individual who captures her audiences with her remarkable humor.

To Sally, *Keeping You in Stitches*® is more than the title of her successful sewing and lecture series – it is the philosophy on which she has based her life. Sally's mission is to treat each and every person as an individual with special talents to be used as stepping stones, not stumbling blocks.

"No matter what adjustments have to be taken at the sewing machine, the importance of an accomplishment by each individual is what matters the most," says Sally.

The columnist and author is an award-winning member of Toastmasters International and is a sought-after lecturer, speaking throughout the United State on topics such as Health and Well Being and Sewing and Motivation. Her fundamental approach to learning is that disabilities (whether real or perceived) are not obstacles, but challenges to be overcome with humor and a positive attitude. This viewpoint is apparent in all of Sally's projects.

Sally invites you to contact her via e-mail at: stitches@aug.com

http://www.keepingyouinstitches.com
Sewing ideas, books, videos, chat room, message board

Resources

Superior Threads

PO Box 1672
St. George, UT 84771
800.499.1777
http://www.superiorthreads.com
www.superiorthreads.com
Large selection of high-quality products such as metallic thread, pre-wound bobbins, Dissolve, glitter

Sulky of America

3113 Broadpoint Dr.
Dept. QB
Harbor Heights, FL 33983
http://www.sulky.com
e-mail: sulkyofamerica@mindspring.com
Threads such as Ultra Twist™, metallic threads, stabilizers, puffy foam, transfer pens, adhesives

Robinson-Anton

PO Box 159
Fairview, NJ 07022
800.932.0250
http://www.robinson-anton.com
e-mail: Rathread@halper.com
Special threads such as Super Strength® Rayon, Twister tweed rayon, Super Brite® polyester, metallic spools, pre-wound bobbins

Babylock U.S.A.

PO Box 730
Fenton, MO 63026
http://www.babylock.com
Complete line of sewing machines, sergers, embroidery/sewing products, line of software and furniture products

Pfaff

Husqvarna Viking
31000 Viking Parkway
Westlake, OH 44145
440.808.6550
http://www.pfaff.com
Complete line of computerized sewing machines, sergers, steam team, and other accessories

Helpful Web Sites

Keeping You in Stitches

http://www.keepingyouinstitches.com
Sewing ideas, books, videos, chat room, message board

Sherwin Williams

http://www.sherwinwilliams.com/diy
Ideas for all sorts of do-it-yourself home improvements, interior or exterior

Decorating Secrets

http://www.decoratingsecrets.com
Decorating secrets, decorating kit, and lots of advice

Baranzelli

http://www.baranzelli.com
Offers an exclusive collections of fabrics, trimmings, and furniture

Home Arts

http://www.homearts.com
Decorating ideas and so much more

Benjamin Moore

http://www.benjaminmoore.com
Advice from designers, homeowners, architects

Our House

http://www.ourhouse.com
A wonderful shopping resource for tools, hardware, appliances, conveniences, and decorator items

Home Depot

http://www.homedepot.com
A resource for so many home improvement ideas – features a section dedicated to decorating projects

Home Central

http://www.homecentral.com
Home remodeling ideas

Corner Hardware

http://www.cornerhardware.com
A place to find hundreds of well-written how-to articles

Index

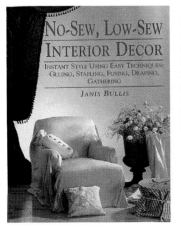

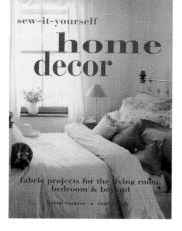

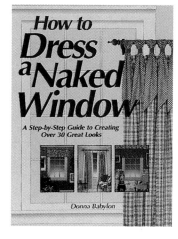

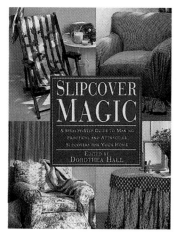

Also by Sally Cowan...

Sew A Beautiful Home
Quick and Easy Home Decorating Projects

by Sally Cowan

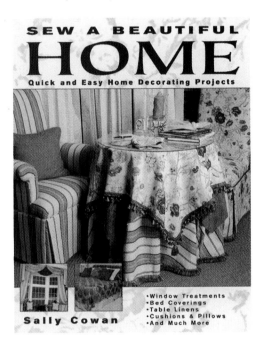

Would you like to add some zip to your decor without spending a lot of time and money? Popular TV personality and home dec expert Sally Cowan can show you how. From simple window treatments and pillows to elegant bed and table covers, Sally's creative ideas and simple instructions help you create a new look for your home. Sally includes projects and ideas for difficult-to-decorate areas such as home offices, hallways, bathrooms, and even motorhomes, as well as the more traditional spaces such as bedrooms and kitchens.

Softcover • 8-1/4 x 10-7/8 • 160 pages

200 illustrations • 250 color photos

Item# SBH • $24.95